CERAMICS FOR BEGINNERS

hand building

CERAMICS FOR BEGINNERS

hand building

Shay Amber

LARK BOOKS

A Division of Sterling Publishing Co., Inc.
New York / London

SENIOR EDITOR: Suzanne J. E. Tourtillott

PRODUCTION EDITOR: Nathalie Mornu

EDITOR: Susan Huxley

ART DIRECTOR: Thom Gaines

PHOTOGRAPHER: Steve Mann

COVER DESIGNER: Cindy LaBreacht

This book is dedicated to my godmother, Lynne Burke, for her steadfast encouragement, love, and support.

Library of Congress Cataloging-in-Publication Data

Amber, Shay.
 Ceramics for beginners : hand building / Shay Amber. -- 1st ed.
    p. cm.
 Includes index.
 ISBN 978-1-60059-243-0 (hc-plc with jacket : alk. paper)
 1. Pottery craft. I. Title.
 TT920.A44 2008
 738.1'4--dc22
                                        2008011404

10 9 8 7 6 5 4 3 2 1

First Edition

Published by Lark Books, A Division of
Sterling Publishing Co., Inc.
387 Park Avenue South, New York, NY 10016

Text © 2008, Shay Amber
Photography © 2008, Lark Books unless otherwise specified
Illustrations © 2008, Lark Books

Distributed in Canada by Sterling Publishing,
c/o Canadian Manda Group, 165 Dufferin Street
Toronto, Ontario, Canada M6K 3H6

Distributed in the United Kingdom by GMC Distribution Services,
Castle Place, 166 High Street, Lewes, East Sussex, England BN7 1XU

Distributed in Australia by Capricorn Link (Australia) Pty Ltd.,
P.O. Box 704, Windsor, NSW 2756 Australia

If you have questions or comments about this book, please contact:
Lark Books
67 Broadway
Asheville, NC 28801
828-253-0467

Manufactured in China

ISBN 13: 978-1-60059-243-0

For information about custom editions, special sales, and premium and
corporate purchases, please contact the Sterling Special Sales Department
at 800-805-5489 or specialsales@sterlingpub.com.

contents

Introduction

I love the feel of clay between my fingers. It's smooth and moist—an elemental material. I like its receptivity, the way it responds to the slightest pressure, retaining marks and textures. That is why I work with clay, and why I'm passionate about sharing what I know.

I TEACH HAND BUILDING CLASSES, AND THIS BOOK IS SET UP JUST LIKE A WORKSHOP, with instructions and step-by-step process photos that offer a simple, informative, and inspired look at the unlimited possibilities of forming clay by hand. *Hand Building* is the first title in the new Ceramics for Beginners series; I wrote it for those who want to learn to make simple yet beautiful ceramic objects.

Unlike wheel throwing, the hand-building methods in this book require little practice. Just enjoy the feel of clay in your hands and be willing to learn as you go. Because the basic information, techniques, and projects in this book are organized from the simplest to the most involved, I encourage you to work from front to back rather than jumping around. Techniques demonstrated in each section build on the skills and knowledge you learned about in previous sections.

You'll learn how to choose and use clay, work with the hand tools used by ceramists, and gain knowledge on handling the equipment. You'll also find information on setting up a safe and efficient workspace. Then it's time to get out a brick of clay and try the simplest technique: pinching. Steps and photos walk you through the general process, then I show you how to create two beautiful forms using just this skill. One is a tea bowl—included because it doesn't require making a perfect shape: A traditional Japanese tea bowl should have imperfections. The other, the Wafer Vase, takes the method in an entirely different direction, showing how little clay wafers, can be combined to make a dramatic piece.

More hand-building techniques follow: coiling, draping slabs, and building with stiff slabs, with fun projects related to each. The coil section, for example, features a set of espresso cups with spiral handles, and in the slab building section, I teach you to make a Carved Lantern. Another section shows how to stamp clay and turn its imprint into an appliqué you can attach to any form, including tiles and sculptural pieces. You also learn to make your own stamps, including one for marking your name on every piece you create. And since the work of others can serve as inspiration, each section is accompanied by a gallery of hand-built work by contemporary ceramists.

Once you have an understanding of the techniques and have developed some skills in each, you're poised for creative exploration. The artistic impulse has always existed alongside the need for functional vessels. You can use hand-built forms to express an amazing array of ideas. I include a section explaining how I bring basic design elements— pattern, shape, and texture—from photos, sketches, and other sources directly into the form and surface of my own work.

The creative journey doesn't end after the forming of a piece; it continues with the decisions you make while decorating, glazing, and firing. The Surface Decoration section gives an overview of some methods for creating visual interest on a piece. You might inscribe the clay; draw lines of thinner clay on the surface; polish the clay to a rich, deep gleam; or add color and depth with glazes. I provide recipes for glazes and other liquid embellishments, and you'll discover fascinating ways to apply a coating as rich or as pale, as matte or glossy, as multilayered or transparent as you like. Finally, I include an overview of the firing process.

With my simple and basic approach to hand building, you can quickly construct both useful objects and sculptural forms, then choose from many decorative methods to make the pieces unique. The rewarding, wonderful world of clay has never been more accessible or easy to understand. Plunge your fingers into a hunk of clay, and get ready to discover your own creative vision.

Choosing and Using Clay

This chapter contains a rough overview of what clay is and the different types of clay that are available to suit your needs. Before you get your hands in the clay, you should understand some of the basics about the material you will be working with.

AN UNDERSTANDING OF BASIC CLAY COMPOSITION will help you choose the best clay for the form that you're making and determine the way that the piece will be embellished and finished. Although the ceramic process involves chemical compounds and changes, you don't need a science degree to understand how clay works or, more importantly, how to get clay to work for you.

Clay is basically a kind of pulverized rock. Ceramists who know what to look for may just dig it out of the bank of a river or stream near their studio. (Specific locations are often closely guarded secrets.) Their troves are usually contaminated with organic and inorganic materials, so they're called *secondary clays*, which are just fine for hand building.

Kaolin is the most common type of a purer (*primary*) clay that ceramists can find. It's difficult to work with because it's dense and *nonplastic* (less pliable). Nevertheless, you'll find kaolin mixed into manufactured clay, particularly porcelain, because it has a low shrinkage rate and it's white. There are lighter, more plastic clays than kaolin, called *ball clays,* but ceramists mix them into other types of clay since they shrink a lot.

You need some experience with clay before you go on your own treasure hunt, because working with clay that you dig up involves quite a bit of experimenting. Your best course of action is to purchase clay until you're comfortable with all of the processes that are part of creating a ceramic piece.

Manufacturers create clay that's formulated with specific qualities for hand building, and probably include helpful information in the packaging. For example, manufacturers usually indicate the clay's *firing range* (the optimum low to high temperatures for heating a piece in a specialty oven, called a *kiln,* until the clay particles compress to make a form that won't dissolve or easily break). The packaging may also indicate what other ingredients are in the clay, called *additives.* These affect the color (see page 10), texture (see page 10), and firing range.

Your first step is choosing a suitable clay, because each type has a unique color, consistency, and firing range.

■ CLAY BODIES

When you shop, you don't look for a primary or secondary clay. Instead, choose earthenware, stoneware, or porcelain. In a class setting, your instructor may have all three types available for you to try because you'll have access to the expertise and equipment to help you succeed. On your own, it's best to work with earthenware until you're established.

EARTHENWARE is the most prevalent—and commonly used—type of secondary clay. The finished piece shown at the start of every project in this book is made from it. Since the firing temperature is low (around 1940°F or 1060°C), this clay is an excellent choice if you're concerned about the effect that high-fire kilns have on the environment or your pocketbook.

It always contains some amount of iron oxide, which accounts for its signature red color. But don't be surprised if you find white earthenware clay. Try it if you want to show off a bright, translucent *glaze* (a liquid that, when applied to a fired clay piece and refired, fuses to the surface and becomes hard and glasslike).

STONEWARE, also a secondary clay, is fired at a much higher temperature than earthenware. Before buying it (or porcelain) make sure that the kiln you're using can get hot enough. At its peak temperature of 2200°F (1204°C), stoneware shrinks and becomes nearly *nonporous* (impervious to water). This clay is perfect for making functional ware that holds food or drink because liquids won't seep through the clay walls. There are many variations of

this clay because stoneware contains metals and minerals that will alter its color from light gray to dark brown when fired.

PORCELAIN, a more refined type of stoneware, is durable. Yet porcelain's white, translucent appearance gives it a delicate, pristine sensibility. Its smooth and creamy consistency feels wonderful and allows the clay to pick up the slightest textural detail. However, its nonplastic quality makes it difficult to work with.

■ COLOR

The firing temperature can dramatically change clay's color. For example, stoneware clay that's gray in the raw state may turn pink in the initial firing, then turn dark gray or even brown after being *glaze-fired* (see page 115).

Glaze can add a new color to your clay or enhance what's already there. However, the clay that you choose for your piece will affect the appearance of the glaze. If you're uncertain how a glaze will look on a white or a red clay, apply the glaze to a sample of each and fire it. If desired, you can lessen the effect of your clay on the glaze by first applying an *underglaze* (see page 91) or a liquid water-clay mixture called *slip* to the surface.

A sand-like material can be mixed into clay for additional texture.

Metals, minerals, and other ingredients affect the color of different clay bodies.

■ TEXTURE

Clay that's formulated for hand building often includes *grog*. This is basically fired clay that has been ground into sandlike particles.

You can buy grog separately and add it to clay, although this isn't an easy process (see Clay Preparation and Storage and Reclaiming on page 13). Most beginners—and many experienced ceramists—simply buy clay with grog mixed into it.

Grog comes in different sizes, or *meshes*. The coarser the mesh, the more texture, or *tooth*, the clay will have after the grog is added. Clays containing large amounts of coarse grog are great for creating tiles or large sculptural forms. On the other hand, if you're making dinnerware choose clay containing finer grog, or no grog at all.

You can create visual texture by working *burnout* materials into clay, such as rice and coffee grounds. When fired, the heat destroys these additives so that the surface of the finished form is pitted.

■ STAGES OF DRYNESS

Some very small pieces can dry naturally, but larger work needs to dry at a slower pace so it doesn't crack, warp, or separate. To control the drying time, place the work under a thin sheet of plastic. If desired, you can cover only the areas that you suspect will dry faster. Punch holes in the plastic if you want the clay to dry at a faster rate. Remove the plastic when the work is almost completely dry.

Ceramists use special terms to describe the relative amount of moisture in clay. Any piece you make will go through four stages of dryness described here before you put it in a kiln to be fired.

MOIST, OR PLASTIC, CLAY is the most malleable state. Fresh out of the bag, moist clay is ideal for constructing pinched or coiled forms because it's soft and pliable. *Wet* is often used to describe the material at this stage, although some ceramists reserve the term for product that has a considerable amount of water in it, such as slip. You can use slip as a glue to join pieces of clay (see page 59) or for surface decoration techniques (see page 90 and 95 to 96).

STIFF CLAY is strong enough to hold its shape, but can still be manipulated. If you tried to make a large piece with moist clay, it could collapse under its own weight. Not so with stiff clay. However, it's more prone to cracking. Handle and manipulate a stiff-clay form with care.

LEATHER-HARD CLAY cracks if you try to bend it. It's the preferred state for clay used to construct rigid forms such as boxes. This technique, called stiff slab construction (see page 58), is possible because leather-hard clay pieces still have enough moisture to be joined.

BONE-DRY CLAY won't get any drier unless it's fired. Forms at this stage are known as *greenware*. Place an unfired clay form on your cheek for five seconds. If the clay feels cold, there's still moisture in it. If the clay is at room temperature, it's bone dry. You can't bend, shape, or join pieces of bone-dry clay.

For hand building, moist clay, fresh out of the bag, is ready for shaping.

Remoistening Clay

Imagine that you want to cut a hole in a leather-hard clay box. It's possible to do so, although you run the risk of damaging the form as you force your needle tool through the material. It's easier if you first *remoisten* the clay to make it softer. Remoistening is also necessary whenever you need to join two clay shapes that are at different stages of dryness. You need to add a bit of moisture to the harder form so that the clay pieces are at the same stage when joined.

You can remoisten stiff or leather-hard clay by spritzing it with water and then placing it under a thin plastic sheet. This is a gentle process that requires a ginger application of water. The last thing you want to do is wet the work down and walk away from it. Instead, evenly mist the clay every 15 minutes,

constantly monitoring the piece until it reaches the desired stage of dryness. It's important to be cautious because overdoing it will cause a piece to warp when it's in the kiln. Also, don't remoisten a bone-dry clay form because it'll just dissolve.

■ BISQUE WARE

After you make a form and let it reach the fragile bone-dry stage, you place it in a kiln and fire it to make it hard. This is the *bisque firing*. The piece that you take out of the kiln is called *bisque ware*. Although some glazes can be applied to greenware, bisque firing is usually needed to prepare the clay for glaze application. This first firing removes any remaining water and harmful gasses that might ruin the glaze. After you apply the glaze, fire the piece a second time at a higher temperature. This *glaze firing* permanently fuses the glaze to the surface of the bisque piece.

After a clay piece is fired for the first time, it's porous enough to accept a glaze.

■ TESTING SHRINKAGE

Clay is at its greatest volume at the wet stage. As it dries, the water that's in it evaporates, and the size of the piece decreases. When the clay is fired, your piece contracts even more. This process is known as *shrinkage*. Different clays shrink at different rates, and the higher the firing temperature, the more the clay will shrink. Some clay bodies, such as earthenware, may only shrink 7 percent. Other clays, including porcelain, shrink as much as 18 percent.

You need to know a clay's shrinkage rate when the finished piece must be a specific size. Manufacturers usually provide the shrinkage rates for their clays fired to a specific temperature. If you mixed grog or other additives into the clay used to make a form, or you plan to fire a clay piece to a different temperature, you need to determine the shrinkage rate yourself. You conduct this test with a clay ruler.

Making a Clay Ruler

Roll a small, ⅜-inch (1 cm) thick slab (see page 47). Use a needle tool to cut it to 2 x 12 inches (5.1 x 30.5 cm), and carve exact measurements into the clay, using a ruler as a guide. Let the clay dry until it's bone dry, and then fire it at the exact temperature that you plan to fire the form you're going to make from the same clay. Apply *patina* to the surface (see page 110) so that you can read the marks. Fire the ruler a second time, again to the same temperature you plan to use for the form.

Attach the clay ruler to a scrap of wood that's cut to the same size, using epoxy glue. Write the type of clay and the firing temperature on the wood.

This finished piece is smaller than the shape you cut from the moist clay, so you can use it to determine the shrinkage of the clay. The simple formula, using an 8-inch-square (20.3 cm) piece as an example, follows.

Subtract the length of the finished clay ruler from the length of the original ruler:
8 inches – 7.25 inches = 0.75 inch
(20.3 - 18.4 cm = 1.9 cm)

Divide this result by the length of the original ruler:
0.75 inch / 8 inches = 0.09
(1.9 cm / 20.3 cm = 0.09)

Multiply this result by 100:
0.09 x 100 = 9

In this example, the clay's shrinkage rate is 9 percent.

A difference in size is clearly visible in this bone-dry clay piece (top) and its fired twin.

■ POROSITY AND VITRIFICATION

When clay is fired, all moisture is removed and the particles are compressed. This process turns the clay into a ceramic medium. Clay that has gone through a higher firing is stronger than the results of a typical lower-temperature first firing for bisque ware. A porous clay can still expand and contract, which could cause the glaze to crack and make it unsafe for food. If you're making a decorative or sculpted piece, such as the Bird Sculpture on page 75, you don't have to worry about clay's porous nature. *Vitrification* is the point at which the clay particles have reached their highest rate of compression. This occurs during the final firing. The hard, vitrified clay is dense and impervious to water.

Water will leak through porous clay (right), while clay fired to vitrification will hold water (left).

As long as it hasn't been fired, any clay can be crumbled, moistened with water, and then reused to make an entirely new form.

STORAGE AND RECLAIMING

Reclaimed clay has a light, plastic consistency that lends itself beautifully to pinched or coiled techniques. Clay should be absolutely bone dry before it's reclaimed. This process creates dust, so it's a good idea to wear a mask or respirator.

First, break up the clay into small pieces and eliminate any lumps. Place the clay in a large bucket and fill it with water until the clay is submerged. It'll quickly absorb water and turn to mush. At this point, experienced ceramists may add grog (see page 10). This can be tricky because an unbalanced ratio of grog can cause cracking and other structural problems.

Once the water appears to be completely absorbed, place the bucket upside down over an old piece of fabric to let the clay drain until it's moist. Wedge it (as described at top right).

Store your clay where it can be kept as moist as possible: away from extreme heat and direct sunlight. When tightly sealed in plastic bags, the clay should keep sufficiently moist for about six months. It's a good idea to monitor the moisture content and spray the clay with water as needed.

Clay, like wine or cheese, improves with age—if it's stored properly. Ceramists actually encourage mold growth on clay because it improves the plasticity. Some ceramists mix organic matter or yogurt into their clay to promote this mold growth. In Japan, clay is sometimes dug up, prepared, and then buried again for future generations to unearth and then use.

CLAY PREPARATION

Ceramists *wedge* clay to loosen it up, make sure that it's well mixed, and to remove air bubbles that could make a form explode when fired. Experienced ceramists also use wedging to introduce grog and other additives to their clay bodies.

The wedging method described here is just one of several that ceramists use.

Soft, moist clay is easier to wedge than stiff clay. If your clay is sticky, let it dry out a bit. Place 8 pounds (3.6 kg) of clay on a nonstick surface that's at hip level. Position your body with one foot pointed straight ahead and the other slightly behind, to act as a brace. Form the clay into a ball. Press your body weight into the ball with one of your palms. Without releasing the clay, cradle and lift the front with the other hand. Push the front down into the clay's center. Repeat this process.

You're finished wedging when all of the air bubbles have been removed. To check for air bubbles, cut through the center of the clay mass with a wire tool. The exposed surfaces should be flat and completely smooth.

Wedge reclaimed clay and clay scraps you plan to reuse.

Getting to Know the Studio

You can enjoy hand building—and protect your health—to a greater degree if your studio is set up appropriately and you have the right tools and equipment. Read on to learn more about setting up your work space, the items that you really need, and things that you can add to a wish list.

ALL THAT YOU REALLY NEED to build a piece are your hands, a chunk of clay, and a worktable. Exquisite ware can emerge with little more. Nevertheless, having some tools and a few pieces of equipment will probably make any process more satisfying. It's also important to establish good habits to keep your studio safe.

■ YOUR WORK AREA

Most communities have ceramic studios where you can take classes or rent space and share equipment and tools at a communal studio. These are great ways to get acquainted with a studio while discovering your creative direction.

If you decide to set aside a personal space for hand building in your home, consider converting a garage or finished basement to help you keep clay dust and other contaminants away from primary living quarters.

A 12 x 15-foot (3.6 x 4.5 m) area can accommodate a worktable, shelves, a slab roller (see page 20), and a medium-size kiln. To avoid dust that can wreak havoc with clay and glazes, the walls, ceiling, and floor need to be smooth and easy to wipe down. The floor should be easy to sweep. Also look for access to running water and good lighting. The worktable should be sturdy enough to withstand significant weight and movement.

■ SAFETY PROCEDURES

A clay studio can be a safe and enjoyable environment if you follow a few precautions when setting it up. Read these procedures before you start hand building.

KEEP A CLEAN STUDIO. You don't want to inhale clay dust. *Silica*, one of clay's main ingredients, can cause a lung disease called silicosis. For cleaner air, install a professional ventilation system. If this isn't an option, choose a studio space with windows or doors that you can open to let fresh air circulate.

You can avoid your doctor's office by developing habits that keep down the dust in your studio: Clean your workstation at the end of each session. Wipe down your tables and equipment with a clean, damp sponge. Sweep the floor with a sweeping compound.

KNOW THE INGREDIENTS. Always read the label on the packaging for any underglaze, glaze, luster, or other material that you plan to use. If the information is skimpy, ask your ceramic supplier for details.

WEAR PROTECTIVE CLOTHING AND GEAR. To avoid tracking dust through your home, designate a pair of shoes for the studio. Pick a closed-toe style to protect your toes. Take these shoes off as you exit your studio. Also wear safety glasses to protect your eyes from heat and radiation as you monitor the progress of the firings while looking into a kiln's peephole.

DISPOSE OF WASTE PROPERLY. Use a bucket to collect residue from glazes, oxide *colorants*, and other harmful chemicals. Once you have a couple of cups of this residue, let it dry completely. Make a ceramic bowl, put the residue in it, and fire it to *cone 6* (see page 117 to learn more about *pyrometric* cones). After firing, you can dispose of the bowl and its contents safely, knowing that the materials will not leach into the ground.

KNOW THE CLAY BODY. If you work with more than one type of clay body, clean your equipment and tools after you use them. Also store moist red and white clay separately.

UNDERSTAND THE EQUIPMENT. Even though most kilns have safety features, they can cause a fire or even an explosion. An operating manual is hardly exciting reading, but do take the time to go through it. Also, never leave the premises while the kiln is firing. Even a new kiln can malfunction. If you're *raku* or *pit firing* (see page 118), make sure all *combustibles* (such as leaves or sawdust) are completely extinguished before leaving the premises.

MONITOR YOUR VISITORS. Pregnant women should consult with their doctors before working in a clay studio—if you're expecting, that means you, too. Supervise children during all ceramic activities.

SEGREGATE YOUR ACTIVITIES. Do not eat, drink, or smoke in the studio. Always wash your hands thoroughly once you're finished working.

It's a good idea to label containers, especially any that hold a medium containing hazardous chemicals.

■ YOUR BASIC TOOL KIT

You can take a quick glance in any ceramic supply catalog or website to confirm that there are many materials, tools, and pieces of equipment for hand building. To help you sort out what you need, here's a list of supplies that you'll use to create every project in this book. They aren't mentioned at the beginning of each project, but you need to have them on hand.

▲ **A banding wheel,** which is basically a lazy Susan on a pedestal, is very important for sculptural work. You place your clay on it and then develop all sides of the form by turning the wheel.

▲ **Buckets and small containers (with lids)** can hold slips, glazes, and other materials. Noncorrosive buckets, plastic in particular, are ideal.

▲ **Chamois cloths and small, natural or synthetic sponges** work well for smoothing and softening. Sponges are also good for cleaning your tools and work space. Keep one handy when you're working with moist clay so that you can wipe off any excess that's sticking to your hands. It's to smooth a surface when there's clay on your hands because clay tends to stick to clay.

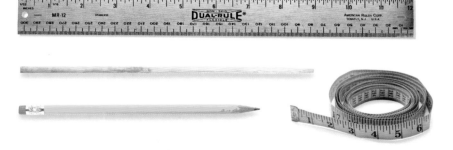

▲ **A metal ruler, pencil, stir stick, and tape measure** have a wide range of uses. Use the tape measure to check the width, length, and depth of curved surfaces. The ruler and pencil will help you cut straight edges for templates (see page 119) and slabs (see page 47).

A flexible straightedge gives you a guide to follow when cutting a straight line along a curved surface. You can make one from a long strip of card stock or a manila folder.

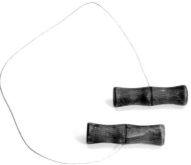

◀ **Slip applicators** are bottles or bulbs that hold liquid and have a tapered tip for applying fine lines of slip, underglaze, and even glaze. Experiment on a test tile, tabletop, or paper until you're comfortable using a slip applicator, and always test the flow before applying it to a piece.

▲ **Rubber gloves** of any type will protect your hands. Always wear them when working with dangerous dry and liquid chemicals.

Plastic sheets help you keep clay moist and control the drying time of a clay piece. The bags placed over dry-cleaned clothes work great because they're large enough to cover most sculptural work.

▲ **Spray bottles** can help you keep clay moist. Just fill a bottle with water and spritz it on the work in progress or the piece that's drying. Intermittently spritz a handle or other appendage with water to ensure it dries at the same rate as the rest of the piece.

▲ **A wire tool** is used to cut a slice or chunk off a block (also known as a brick) or large section of clay. You can make your own wire tool by tying a wood dowel or large washer to each end of a 12-inch length (30.5 cm) of 18-gauge wire. Hold a dowel or washer in each hand and simply pull it through the clay.

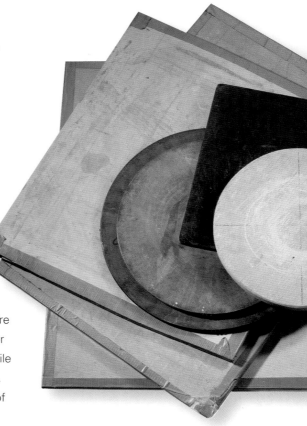

▶ **Ware boards** are flat, mobile work surfaces. It's a good idea to have several, in a variety of sizes. To make your own, see page 25. Bats serve the same function as ware boards, and they'll keep an object moist while you work on it. They're smaller and made from wood, plaster, or plastic. Work on a ware board or bat while creating any of the projects in this book. Choose one that's suitable for the size of the piece that you're making.

▲ **A respirator** is essential in any studio. For your good health, you must wear it when working around any dry ceramic chemical, including clay dust, even if your studio has a ventilation system. If you're on a tight budget, a basic dust mask will suffice. If you find yourself spending hours at a time in the studio, invest in your health: Buy that respirator!

■ OTHER ESSENTIALS

At the beginning of each project, there are photos of additional tools you'll need to collect to make the featured piece. While you learn which techniques and tools speak to you, purchase the following only as needed. You can often improvise with common household objects. For example, an old fork works great for scoring a clay surface.

▲ **Canvas cloths** are helpful for soft slab construction. Keep at least four canvas cloths in your studio so that you can dedicate one set for use with dark clay and another for light clay. This prevents cross-contamination of the clays.

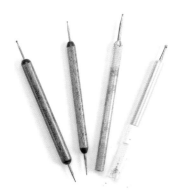

▲ **Ball stylus tools** are perfect for drawing into the clay surface. The tip makes a wider line than the tip of a needle tool. Collect several sizes so you can create a range of line types in your clay.

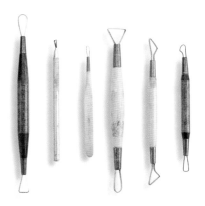

▲ **Loop tools** are great for trimming or carving away clay, as in the sgraffito surface decoration technique (see page 93). When you build your tool collection, include several with loops of various sizes.

▲ **A mitering tool** is dragged along the edge of a clay slab to create a 45° angle. When you cut such an angle in the adjacent edges of two separate slabs, they can be joined with an attractive seam (see page 59). See page 24 to learn how to make your own mitering tool.

▲ **Needle tools** are used to cut through clay. To start, you only need one. This pencil-like implement is great for cutting narrow angles and curved lines. You may not need one if you only want to pinch or coil forms (see pages 26 and 34).

▲ **Metal hole makers** are available in different diameters. They make perfectly round holes in the clay for functional as well as decorative purposes. In a pinch, you can make a hole with a needle tool.

▲ **Rubber-tipped tools** all have soft flexible tips. With these, you can make beautiful organic drawings or add surface detail to moist clay.

▼ **Scoring tools** create the toothy surface needed to join pieces of clay (see page 59). To cover a large area quickly, opt for the long surface of a serrated metal rib. When scoring small areas, a wire brush or a kitchen fork will do the trick.

▼ **A rolling pin** makes it possible for you to hand roll a clay slab. Find the longest one possible so that you can make a wide slab. Clay sticks to marble so it's best to use a wooden rolling pin.

▲ **Ribs** are used to shape and smooth clay walls. Metal ribs cause *grog* (see page 10) to rise to the clay's surface, so they're best used on clay that contains little or no grog. Wooden ribs are stiff and strong, to provide the most resistance when altering the shape of a wall. They leave subtle natural texture on the clay. Rubber ribs come in various degrees of flexibility. Soft rubber ribs conform to curved areas. A rigid rubber rib has enough strength to shape a wall while rendering a smooth surface.

▼ **Paintbrushes** are used to apply slip, underglaze, and glaze. Collect an assortment that includes the thinnest liner brush to much wider ones. For a smoother, more efficient application, choose soft, natural bristles that hold a lot of liquid. Use a sponge or foam brush to apply a wax resist (see page 109).

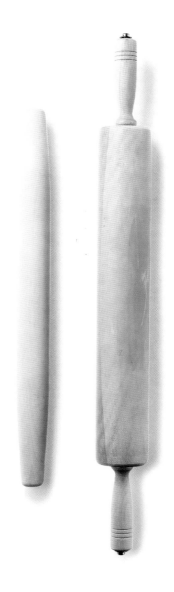

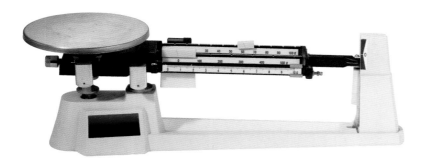

▲ **A scale** measures ingredients for ceramic recipes. Choose one that measures in grams, pounds, and kilograms.

▶ **An electric mixer or blender** comes in handy for mixing slips, washes, and glazes. If you get a power drill mixer attachment, select one that's safe for plastic containers.

▲ **Wooden modeling tools** allow you to refine areas and achieve greater detail. They're helpful reaching into areas you can't access with your fingers. Metal dental tools also work well.

▼ **A slab roller** makes flat sheets of clay, called slabs, to a specific, even thickness. These pieces are used in a type of shaping called slab construction. You can make slabs by hand, but a slab roller is easier and faster, and the results are impressive. You can see a slab roller in action, and learn how it works, on page 48.

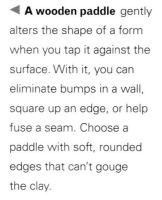

◀ **A wooden paddle** gently alters the shape of a form when you tap it against the surface. With it, you can eliminate bumps in a wall, square up an edge, or help fuse a seam. Choose a paddle with soft, rounded edges that can't gouge the clay.

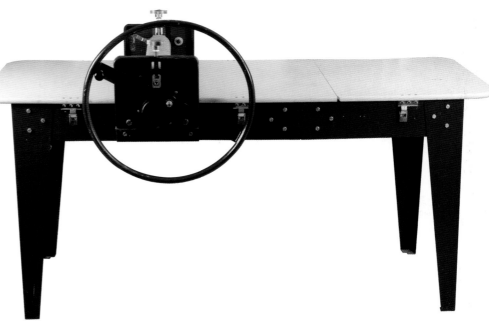

Clockwise from far left, a rectangular hump mold, a press mold with decorative surface, a bowl-shaped slump mold, and an antique cookie mold used as a sprig mold, with a molding made from it

From front to back, a white plaster porous mold, an orange bisque-fired mold, and a clear plastic nonporous mold

Molds

You can make the same shape over and over again, or create only one of a specific shape, with a mold. This section describes types of molds, as categorized by shape and the material they're made of. Some ceramic supply stores sell molds, and you can make your own using simple household shapes (see the Footed Bowl on page 49). Ceramists can even create their own molds by casting shapes with plaster.

If you use a household object, watch out for *undercuts*. These are angles on a mold that trap clay, making it impossible for the mold to release clay.

HUMP MOLDS allow you to shape a form by placing clay over the exterior (or convex side). Since the outside of your clay form is exposed while it's on the mold, you can add attachments like handles or feet.

PRESS MOLDS are often used in tile production, or for pieces that are flat or two-dimensional. You press clay into the concave surface. *Sprig* molds are a type of press mold.

SLUMP MOLDS allow you to work inside pieces while they're on the mold because clay is placed on the inner, concave surface. Most slump and hump molds are used to shape soft slabs (see page 46).

BISQUE-FIRED MOLDS are lightweight, porous, and can be used as both slump and hump molds. As the name implies, they're just clay that has been hardened by firing to the bisque stage.

POROUS MOLDS are the easiest type to use. They're usually made of wood, plaster, or unglazed clay. You simply place clay onto the mold. The porous surface absorbs moisture from the clay, which allows it to set quicker than it would on a nonporous surface.

NONPOROUS MOLDS are made of material such as glass, metal, or glazed clay. Wet clay sticks to these surfaces, first cover the mold with a sheet of plastic to prevent the clay from adhering.

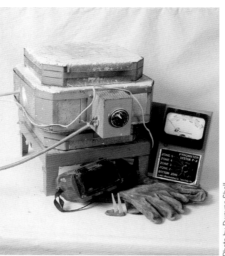

Photo by Dwayne Shell

Kilns range from primitive to electric.

■ KILNS

Kilns are essential for completing the ceramic process. They're classified according to their type of fuel: electric, gas, wood; or design, such as one of the many Japanese-style hand-built kilns; or even by process, as for the quick-fire method called raku.

ELECTRIC KILNS offer a wide firing range. Once programmed, they can practically fire themselves—but never leave one unattended!

Beginners usually start with an electric kiln, which is used to fire clay to the bisque stage and also to fire glaze coatings to maturity. A staple in ceramic studios, an electric type is relatively economical to purchase and operate,

and offers a clean and efficient firing solution. Shapes and sizes vary. Smaller ones—about the size of a microwave— are perfect for firing small pieces or glaze tests. Kilns are also available in models the size of a refrigerator, or even bigger. Since larger kilns take a while to fill with work, start with a small- to medium-size one. That way, you can experiment and fire your work more frequently, and you'll develop your skill and style much more quickly.

Since electric kilns are portable, they're also a great solution for the home studio. Remember that clays and glazes emit potentially toxic gasses when firing, though, so your kiln

should ideally reside in its own room. If separate quarters aren't an option, invest in a ventilation system to remove dangerous fumes.

GAS KILNS come in many different sizes. They're capable of firing at high temperatures, up to cone 13. These fuel-burning kilns run on everything from natural gas or propane to biofuels. Unlike their electric counterpart, gas kilns are able to perform a *reduction firing*, a process that reduces the amount of oxygen in the kiln's atmosphere to affect the color of some clays and glazes.

Due to its large size and the amount of fuel required, the gas kiln is probably more suitable for the advanced ceramic artist who wishes to create the special effects that can be achieved by gas firing. Many community studios offer classes that give the beginner some experience with this process.

WOOD KILNS typically consist of a large *chamber* (interior) that burns at least a cord of wood in a single firing. A firing can take 20 to 30 hours and requires constant monitoring. The *anagama*, or cave kiln, is an extremely large type of wood-fueled kiln that sometimes takes weeks to fire.

▶ **Tip:** If you want to buy a kiln, also consider purchasing shelves, posts, and stilts so that you can fit more pieces inside and protect them from glaze problems.

■ MAKING AND USING TEMPLATES

Several of the projects in this book are made with flat clay shapes that are cut from slabs. All you need to make a template for a project are sheets of cardstock (or some manila folders), a mat knife, glue or carbon paper, and access to a photocopier. Some templates are simple shapes that you can draw with the dimensions provided in the project instructions, in which case you don't need a photocopier.

Photocopy the selected templates, which start on page 119. Still at the photocopier, enlarge or reduce all of them the same amount to create full-size shapes that, when cut from clay and assembled, create a form of the desired size. Make sure that the templates aren't so large that the finished clay piece doesn't fit in your kiln.

Cut out the photocopies and trace them onto cardstock. Now cut the cardstock to the template shapes, using the mat knife. You only need one template for each shape. The labels and project instructions tell you the number of clay shapes you need to cut with each template.

If you want to be able to reuse the templates, first apply shellac or spray paint to make them water resistant.

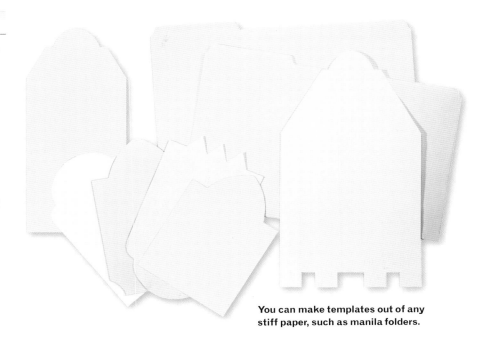

You can make templates out of any stiff paper, such as manila folders.

Place the templates on a clay slab that's large enough to accommodate them and then cut them out, using a needle tool. The pressure of cutting creates resistance, potentially stretching and distorting the desired shape, so be patient. Make several incisions rather than cutting all the way through in one pass. Start from the outside corner and cut toward the center.

Use templates to cut shapes with a confident hand. Spread your fingers to stabilize the template when cutting around it. If you must move your hand to a new spot on a large template, don't lift your fingertips off the surface. Instead, walk your hand to the new position by bringing your thumb into the fingertips and then shift the fingers without moving the thumb.

■ MAKING STUDIO TOOLS

You can buy every important tool that you need for hand building. Nevertheless, you can save money by easily making some yourself. The following pages explain how to make a ware board, mitering tool, and shims for a slab roller. These will come in handy when you're constructing the projects in this book. To make your own stamps and wire cutter see pages 68, 69, and 17, respectively.

Mitering Tool

This is a useful tool if you want to work with stiff slabs to make square or rectangular forms such as the Nesting Box (see page 79) and Geometric Vessel (see page 60). When you join sides of slabs, you want their edges to meet at a 45° angle. Drawing a mitering tool along an edge easily creates this angle.

If you have a saw, staple gun, pliers, and wire cutters, you can make a mitering tool with a 5-inch (12.7 cm) length of 26-gauge wire and scrap of wood that's 5 x 2½ x ¾ inches (12.7 x 6.4 x 1.9 cm). Remove a corner of the wood block with two 1-inch (2.5 cm) cuts. Make sure the cuts are straight—and perpendicular to the wood edge—so that they meet to form a 90° angle. **1**

Secure the wire to the wood with some staples. Make sure that you cut off the excess wire so that there aren't any exposed rough edges. **2**

Shims

Shims are scraps of wood, cut to specific widths, used to space slab rollers a fixed width apart.

You can create your own set of shims using a saw, drill, and ⅜-inch (1 cm) drill bit. Start by collecting wood pieces in a variety of thicknesses. (Wood shops often give away small scraps.) Cut the scraps down to widths ranging from 2 to 4 inches (5 to 10.2 cm) wide and 5 inches (12.7 cm) long. Write the thickness on each one, and drill a hole in one end. String the shims together on a length of twine or rope.

Drywall Ware Boards

Many materials, such as wood or plastic, are used for ware boards, but drywall is one of the most popular surfaces. It's easy to find at home improvement and hardware stores, and a standard 4 x 8-foot (1.2 x 2.4 m) *sheet*, or section, is inexpensive. If you only need one or two ware boards, ask a store employee about damaged sheets, which are sold at a fraction of the cost of a full sheet. Simply cut off the damaged areas and salvage the rest.

Cutting drywall is very easy with a metal ruler and mat knife. You just place the ruler on the drywall and then draw the knife along the edge of the ruler two or three times to score the surface. You don't have to press hard.

> ▶ **Tip:** Avoid injury by cutting away from your body.

Now place the drywall on a table with the scored mark at the table's edge. Tap with quick force along the scored line to make a clean break through the plaster that's inside the drywall. Complete the break by cutting through the paper coating on the underside. When all sides are cut, cover the exposed edges with duct tape.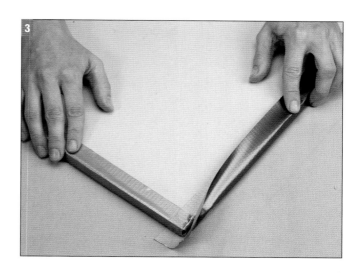

Most Efficient Way of Getting Wareboards from One Sheet of Drywall

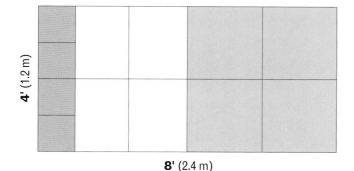

4' (1.2 m)

8' (2.4 m)

Key

- ▢ **1'** (0.3 m) square ware boards
- ▢ **2' x 1½'** (0.6 x 0.5 m) work surface or ware board
- ▢ **2'** (0.6 m) square work or drying surface

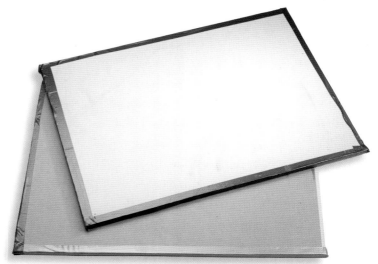

> ▶ **Tip:** Cut drywall far away from any space where you work on clay. Clay work that's contaminated with plaster (or even plaster dust!) will probably explode during the firing.

Technique: **Pinching**

What could be simpler than pushing and pulling on a chunk of clay? Despite the humble nature of this age-old process, called *pinching*, you can make some amazing forms with it. Ceramists often use the same method for pinching a pot, as described here, to create a sculptural form.

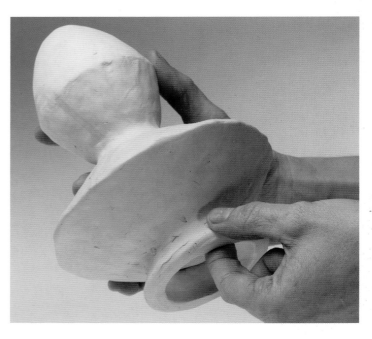

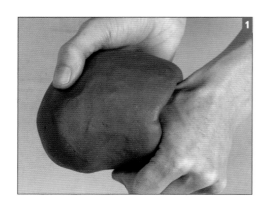

Start by rolling a handful of clay into a ball and then insert the thumb of your dominant hand halfway into it. **1** (Set the clay aside to dry a bit if it's too sticky.) Rotate the ball while it's cupped in your other hand, at the same time pinching the clay between your fingers and thumb. You want to enlarge the center opening while thinning the clay to form the walls. Pinching around the ball opening shifts some of the clay upward, as well as thins the sides to create a wall.

Thin the bottom of the form by pinching it out to the desired width before the wall is too tall. Stop thinning when the bottom and walls are the same thickness. You can reshape the walls if they distort during this process. Now pinch the clay wall to make the opening wider. At the same time, pinch it upward to give the wall more height. **2**

The type of clay and amount of grog in it affects the wall strength. You don't want it so thin that it collapses. Make sure that the wall is smooth and an even width. A small pot does well with a ⅜-inch-thick (1 cm) wall. If a spot is too thin, place a wad of clay on it while the entire form is still moist. Stroke the edges of the patch with your fingers or thumb to fuse it to the wall. Leave the rim a little thicker until most of the form is finished. This prevents it from tearing or cracking. If desired, smooth the rim with a moistened chamois cloth.

Project: **Tea Bowl**

Here's a project that you can approach fearlessly because the finished form doesn't have to be perfect. In fact, asymmetry is part of this piece's charm. When it comes to the tradition of tea bowls, imperfections are encouraged—and even celebrated—in the traditions of the Japanese culture.

1 Insert your thumb into an orange-size ball of clay. This amount will yield a tea bowl that's 3 inches (7.6 cm) tall and has a rim diameter of 4¾ inches (12.1 cm). Begin rotating and pinching to shape the wall. First focus on opening the wall by pinching the clay evenly with your fingers and thumb. Continue pinching until the wall is ½ inch (1.3 cm) thick and 2½ inches (6.4 cm) tall. Keep the bottom 1 inch (2.5 cm) thick.

▶ **Tip:** If you make a tall, narrow tea bowl, use a blunt-edged wooden modeling tool to shape and smooth the interior.

RELATED TECHNIQUES

Glaze Preparation	Dipped Ware	Firing
109–110	**111**	**115**

2 Turn the piece upside down. Pinch out the clay at the bottom to form a ring that has a diameter of 2¼ inches (5.7 cm). Make sure that it's centered. This ring forms the base, or foot, of the tea bowl. Make the foot as even as possible. Place the bowl on a flat surface to assess the bottom of the foot. If necessary, reshape the foot so that it's flat and rests evenly on the table. Turn the bowl right side up. Use your fingertips and thumb to pinch the clay wall in an upward motion, stretching the clay toward the palm of your hand to create a wide, shallow bowl. Stop when the wall is 3 inches (7.6 cm) tall.

3 Smooth the walls and rim with your hands and a dampened chamois cloth. Hold the bowl to ensure it sits comfortably in your hands. Place the bowl on a banding wheel, and give it a 360° turn to inspect the shape. Fine-tune the shape, if needed. Add surface decoration, glaze, and fire as desired. The finished bowl shown on page 27 was coated with a low-fire, opaque white glaze.

A vintage ceramic decal (an image made from china paints that's transferred onto a glaze-fired surface and fired again) is an easy way to add delicate details to a piece.

Project: **Wafer Vase**

This simple vessel allows you to become fluent with pinching by shaping wafers that are subsequently layered to make a form. You'll also be finessing your fusing technique. Use a slow, methodical approach so that you can carefully study the piece as you develop its shape to the final form.

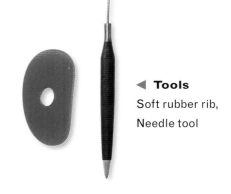

◀ **Tools**
Soft rubber rib,
Needle tool

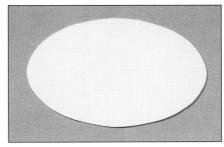

1 Make a template for a base from cardstock. The finished vase was built on a 6 x 3½-inch (15.2 x 8.9 cm) oval.

RELATED TECHNIQUES

Making and Using Templates	Underglaze Application	Patina
23	91	110

2 Pinch a wad of clay about the size of a cherry between your index finger and thumb while rotating it with your other hand. Continue until you have a wafer-shaped piece that's ⅜ inch (1 cm) thick, with the edge tapered to ¼ inch (6 mm) thick. Make enough wafers to fit the base. Also make some for the wall. Place all of the wafers on a ware board under a thin plastic sheet. Spritz them with water to keep them moist, if needed. You can make more wafers as your piece develops.

3 Remove the plastic and place several wafers on a ware board so that the edges slightly overlap and radiate out. Continue until the overlapped wafers are slightly larger than the base. While the clay is still moist, fuse (smooth) the overlapped edges of the pieces together with your fingertips. Make this slab an even width.

4 Smooth the slab's surface with the soft rubber rib. Release (lift) the slab from the ware board without distorting the shape, and then replace it. Place the template on top of the slab. Steady it with your hand. Move the tip of the needle tool through the clay, following the edge of the template until the base is cut from the slab.

5 Place a row of wafers around the perimeter of the base, overlapping the edges as you position them. From the interior, smooth the edges together as you place each wafer. Continue adding rows of wafers in the same manner. Always overlap the wafers' edges the same amount to create an even pattern. Make sure the edges are overlapped far enough to make a wall that's thick enough to prevent the form from collapsing. Stop when the wall is the desired height.

6 Slide the soft rubber rib over the interior of the vase to smooth the large areas. Do this while pressing your other hand on the outside of the wall to match the position of the rib on the interior. Patch thin areas of the wall. Pinch out areas that are too thick. Ideally, the wall should be ¼ to ⅜ inch thick (6 mm to 1 cm). The finished piece shown on page 29 was painted with multiple colors of underglaze (see page 91) while at the greenware stage. Once the piece was bisque fired, a patina (see page 110) was applied using a metallic black low-fire glaze.

A patina emphasizes the overlapping edges of the wafers.

■ Pinched Gallery

Thomas Kerrigan
Desert Sunset IV, 2007

10 x 17½ inches (25.4 x 44.5 cm)
Pinched and slab-built earthenware;
stains, glazes; electric fired
Photo by Wilson Graham

Janis Mars Wunderlich
Portrait of a Puppy, 2006

24 x 12 x 10 inches (61 x 30.5 x 25.4 cm)
Earthenware; slips, underglaze, glaze;
multi-fired in electric kiln
Photo by Jerry Anthony Photography

Alice Ballard
Magnolia Pod, 2000

9 x 14 x 8 inches (22.9 x 35.6 x 20.3 cm)
Hand-built white earthenware;
terra sigillata; electric fired
Photo by artist

Penney Bidwell
Mother, Daughter, 2007

Each, 8 x 6 x 5 inches (20.3 x 15.2 x 12.7 cm)
Pinched, low-fire clay; slips, stains; multi-fired
Photo by John Bonath

Hong-Ling Wee
Dream Stones II, 2005

Each, 2½ x 3 x 3 inches (6.4 x 7.6 x 7.6 cm)
Pinched porcelain; colored slips, clear glaze;
electric fired
Photo by artist

Jill Allen
Vitrafeeler, 2007

7 x 12 x 5 inches (17.8 x 30.5 x 12.7 cm)
Pinched and slab-built earthenware; low-fire
glazes; electric fired; wire added
Photo by artist

Technique: **Forming Coils**

Ropelike strips of clay, called coils, can be wrapped to create flat or dimensional forms, or used to reinforce part of a clay piece. Left exposed on a form, coils create an organic, textured surface that expresses the primitive beauty of the hand-built form. Use larger coils for the thicker walls that big forms need. For an average form, aim for a ⅜-inch-diameter (1 cm) coil.

A hand-pressed coil can forever hold the mark your fingers leave on it, even after the coil is rolled into a shape.

■ HAND PRESSING A COIL

This method involves squeezing the clay into a long, tapered shape. If hand building is new to you, you'll probably find this easier than rolling a coil (see page 35).

Start with a handful of clay. Squeeze it in your hand until it's a rough cylinder. **1** Now rotate your hand so that you're holding the clay vertically. In this position, gravity will help with the shaping. Squeeze out and pull the clay with your other hand. **2** Slide your hands up and down the entire length in order to keep the growing coil an even width throughout.

ROLLING A COIL

This technique usually requires a little practice, but once perfected you'll be able to do it with your eyes closed. Don't use this method simply because it's easier. Choose it because the smooth coil is most suitable for the form you're making.

Squeeze a handful of clay into a thick cylinder. Place the cylinder on a ware board, and position the palm of your hand on top of the center of the cylinder. **3** Start rolling with your hand in the center; as the coil grows longer, use both hands. Shift them outward along the coil's length as you roll back and forth to stretch and thin the clay into a coil. **4** Don't use your knuckles; they'll make the coil uneven.

A hand-rolled coil, shown here after it's wrapped to make a base for a form, is smoother and more even than one that's hand pressed.

It's best to use the palms of your hands because they have a bit more padding, which allows you to exert even pressure for a smoother coil. You want to press hard enough to force the cylinder into a longer shape without leaving fingerprints in the clay.

If the coil does become uneven, apply more pressure to the thicker area as you roll it. If the coil becomes flat, tap it into a rounder shape. **5**

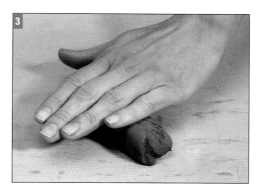

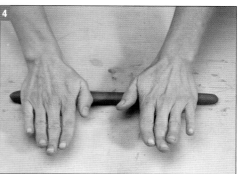

WORKING WITH COILS

It's most likely that you'll need more than one coil to make a form. In this case, you need to taper the ends of each coil so that they can be overlapped when a new length is added during the hand building. When overlapping ends to start a new coil, taper the coil ends to ½ inch long (1.3 cm).

Coils don't have to be the same length. In fact, it's best to use a variety of lengths to make a form because the place where new coils are added shouldn't be adjacent to one another or line up vertically.

If you make a batch of coils, keep them moist under a thin plastic sheet, on a ware board, until you're ready to use each one. It's most important that the coils are moist when they're applied to an emerging form so that they're well fused to one another. If not, the form will fall apart as it dries.

If a coil becomes too long to handle, cut it (or pinch and pull it apart) to create two lengths that you can easily manage.

Project: **Espresso Cup Set**

This set is a great way to develop a sense of proportion between the cup and its handle and to practice creating identical forms. You don't see the coils that were used to build each piece because the sides and ends of each coil were blended.

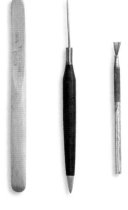

▲ **Tools**
Round-edged
wood modeling
tool, needle tool,
scoring tool

1 Make a batch of coils, each one with a diameter of ¼ inch (6 mm). Taper both ends of each coil, and keep all of them moist under a thin plastic sheet on a ware board until you're ready to use them. Roll a 9-inch-long (22.9 cm) coil into a spiral that has a diameter of 2 inches (5 cm). This is the base for the first cup.

▶ **Tip:** When making several round identical forms, measure the diameter of the first base and make all the rest the same size.

RELATED TECHNIQUES

2 Stroke the surface of the spiral with your thumb and fingertips. Start in the center and work out. You shouldn't be able to see the separate coils when finished blending the surface. Release (lift) the base from the ware board without distorting the shape, and turn it over. In the same manner, fuse and smooth the other side of the spiral. If you inadvertently distorted the spiral, tweak the shape.

3 Place one end of a coil at the outer edge on top of the base, and smooth the tapered end to the base. Press the rest of the coil gently around the perimeter of the base. Continue the coil on top of the first layer. Add more coils—one at a time, overlapping and fusing the tapered ends. Once a couple of layers are in place, smooth the inside wall using your index finger, while bracing the adjacent exterior with your other hand.

4 Continue adding coils and fusing them until the vertical wall is 3 inches (7.6 cm) tall. Stroke the inside and outside of the wall with a round-edged wooden modeling tool. Use vertical strokes and gentle pressure to fuse the coils and make a smooth surface.

5 Smooth the upper edge, or lip, of the cup with your moist fingers. The lip must be smooth so that it will be comfortable against your lips. If your clay contains grog, be careful not to overwork the surface because this will make the lip rougher. Set this cup aside under a thin plastic sheet, spritzing it with water (if necessary) to keep it moist. Make the remaining cups.

6 Make a coil ¼ x 4 inches (6 mm x 10.2 cm). Taper one end and make a small spiral at the other end of the coil. Measure 1½ inches (3.8 cm) from the spiral, and use the needle tool to cut off the end at a 45° angle. Shape the coil into an S curve. This is the handle.

7 Let the sections dry to the stiff stage. Score one of the cups and the handle where they'll be attached. Use the slip trailing applicator to apply slip to all of the scored surfaces. Press the handle to the cup. Wipe off any excess slip, and smooth the place where the handle meets the cup. Complete the remaining cups. The finished pieces shown in the photo on page 36 have a creamy, semiopaque glaze that highlights the subtle textural detail. The finishing touches are low-fire, insect-motif decals (images made from china paints and transferred onto a fired glazed surface and fired again).

The delicate spiral handles acknowledge the origin of these little forms.

Project: **Coiled Bottle**

This bottle is fun to build because you gradually add coils. Centering each new coil on top of the previous one will create a straight wall, but shifting the new coil in or out changes the direction that the wall is growing. To finish the piece, these coils are roughly blended to create a crude yet elegant exterior.

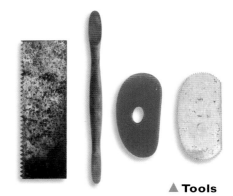

▲ **Tools**

Scoring tool, flat-end and round-edged wood modeling tool, soft rubber rib, metal serrated rib.

1 Roll out a batch of coils, each one with a diameter of ⅜ inch (1 cm). Taper both ends of every coil, and keep all of them moist under a thin plastic sheet until you're ready to use them. Take out one coil and wrap it around itself to make a spiral. Continue adding coils until the spiral's diameter is 4 inches (10.2 cm). This circle is the base. Stroke the surface with your thumb and fingertips, starting in the center and working out. Lift the base off the ware board without distorting the shape, and turn it over. In the same manner, fuse and smooth the remaining side of the spiral.

RELATED TECHNIQUES

Working with Coils	Rolling a Coil	Glazing
35	**35**	**106**

2 Press and fuse a coil on top of the base's perimeter. Continue adding coils—one at a time—on top of the first, overlapping the tapered ends. The place where new coils are added shouldn't line up vertically. This way you avoid creating weak spots. Layering coils vertically in this manner forms the wall of the bottle. Add enough coils to make the wall 3 inches (7.6 cm) high.

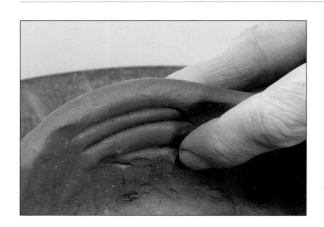

3 Fuse together the coils on the inside of the wall by stroking in a downward motion with your index finger. You're applying pressure to the wall, so brace the outside at the same position with your other hand. Continue adding and fusing coils until the wall is 8 inches (20.3 cm) tall, which is high enough for you to start shaping the shoulder (the top, below the neck).

4 Place the next coil on top of the previous one, but shift it in toward the center to narrow the wall for the start of the shoulder. Continue adding coils that shift inward. As the opening narrows, fuse the coils more frequently, while you still have access to the interior of the piece. When the opening has a 2½-inch (6.4 cm) diameter, let the piece dry until this section is at the stiff stage.

▶ **Tip:** Use a cylinder at least 6 inches (15.2 cm) long to make the bottle's neck. Select an appropriate diameter after you complete the body in step 4, in case the opening isn't exactly 2½ inches (6.4 cm) across.

5 Wind coils into a cylinder that's 4 inches (10.2 cm) tall and has a diameter of 2½ inches (6.4 cm). Fuse the inside with the round-edged wooden modeling tool. Let the neck dry to the stiff stage. Score the bottom of the neck and the top of the bottle where you'll be attaching them.

6 Apply slip to both scored surfaces with a slip applicator, and press the neck to the bottle. Remove the excess slip, and fuse the inside with the wooden modeling tool. Use your fingers to fuse and smooth the exterior seam where the neck joins the tapered bottle opening, while bracing the interior with the fingers of your opposite hand.

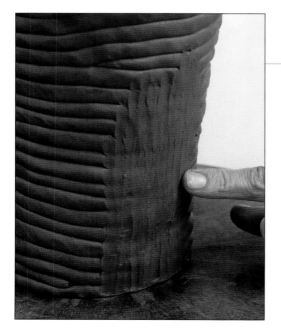

7 To accentuate the texture and reinforce the adhesion of the coils, run your fingers vertically over the exterior surface. Fire and finish your bottle as desired.

When selecting a glaze, consider one that highlights the texture of the coiled walls, such as this green semiopaque glaze.

Coiled Gallery

Jenny Mendes
Birds, 2006

18 x 4 x 4 inches (45.7 x 10.2 x 10.2 cm)
Coiled, pinched terra cotta; terra sigillatas, glaze; electric fired
Photo by Tom Mills

Debra Fritts
Three Women Praying, 2006

34 x 24 x 24 inches (86.4 x 61 x 61 cm)
Hand-built terra cotta; layering slips, oxides,
underglaze, glaze; electric fired, multi-fired
Photo by David Gulisano

Edwards Harper
Heavy Handed, 2006

16 x 10 x 20 inches (40.6 x 25.4 x 50.8 cm)
Press molded, coiled red earthenware;
found objects; electric fired
Photo by Steve Mann

Carol Gentithes
Nosy Be, 2006

25 x 12 x 20 inches (63.5 x 30.5 x 50.8 cm)
Hand-built porcelain mix; coils, slabs, stains, and
silkscreen photo emulsions; electric fired, multi-fired
Photo by Tim Ayers

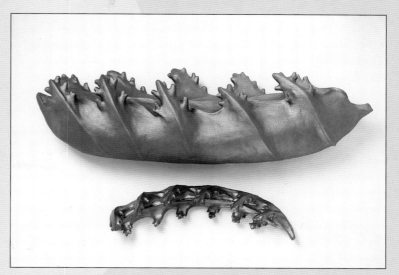

Juan Granados
Sprigs, 2002

25 x 37½ x 7 inches (63.5 x 95.3 x 17.8 cm)
Slab, hand-built earthenware; glaze; electric fired
Photo by J.Q. Thompson

Lars Westby
Untitled, 2005

40 x 18 x 18 inches (101.6 x 45.7 x 45.7 cm)
Hand-built, coiled, and pressed earthenware;
glazed; electric fired
Photo by artist

James Tisdale
Monkey See (Kinetic), 2004

42 x 24 x 24 inches (106.7 x 61 x 61 cm)
Coil-built earthenware; electric fired, cone 03; multi-fired glazes
and underglazes; found objects
Photo by Chris Zaleksy

Lisa Clague
In the Nature of Things, 2004

75 x 48 x 16 inches (190.5 x 121.9 x 40.6 cm)
Coil-built; metal, glazes, stains, wax; cone 04
Photo by Tom Mills

Kerry Jameson
Two Sitting Bull Terriers, 2004

14⅛ x 10¼ x 8⅔ inches (36 x 26 x 22 cm)
Coil-built grogged buff; electric fired, 1100°F (593°C);
slips, glaze 1060°F (571°C)
Photo by Howie

Arthur Gonzalez
The Horizon is Sitting Beside You, 2002

52 x 27 x 13 inches (132 x 69 x 33 cm)
Coil-built ceramic; horsehair, rope, natural sponge, rabbit's foot,
twine, glaze, epoxy, gold leaf
Photo by John Wilson White

Wesley L. Smith
Arachnoid, 2000

8 x 12 x 26 inches (20.3 x 30.5 x 66 cm)
Slab- and coil-built white stoneware; electric fired, cone 04; glaze,
luster, enamel paint, human hair
Photo by artist

Holly Walker
Untitled, 2000

9 x 9¼ x 9¼ inches (22.9 x 23.5 x 23.5 cm)
Pinched earthenware coils; single fired cone 04
Photo by Tom Mills

Fran Welch
Pan, 2007

8 x 9 x 3 inches (20.3 x 22.9 x 7.6 cm)
Lisa Clague, white earthenware; slab, coiled, pinched; high fire
wire; Mason stains, copper wash; crawl glaze; electric fired;
encaustic, beeswax; steel chain and nails
Photo by Steve Mann

Technique: **Making Slabs**

Clay is remarkable: sturdy after firing, yet flexible enough to be draped like fabric when wet. You can take advantage of these characteristics by building strong functional or decorative forms from flexible sheets of clay, called soft slabs. To make the most efficient use of your time and energy, use at least a third of a brick of clay to make a slab. This section describes two basic methods for creating a slab: tossing (also called throwing) and rolling.

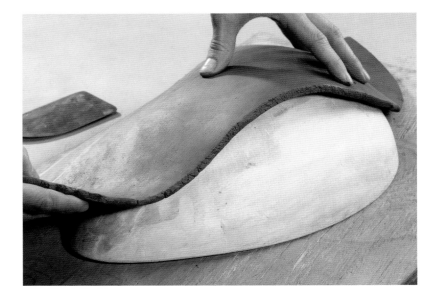

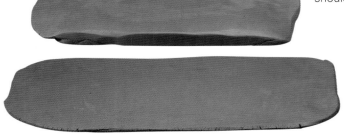

A chunk of clay can be tossed repeatedly to form a slab as thick or as thin as you like.

■ TOSSING

Tossing is the simplest, most low-tech method to form a slab. All you need are strong arms and a flat, nonstick work surface such as a drywall ware board (explained on page 25).

Tossed slabs are best suited for the kind of organic forms you get from hump and slump molds because the clay particles are repeatedly curved during the tossing. Organic forms are more forgiving of slight shifts in shape during drying and firing. In other words, don't toss a slab if you're planning to build a flat-plane form such as a tile or box.

Start with a slice that's no more than a third of a brick: Cut an 8-pound (3.6 kg) slice of clay from a brick with your wire-cutting tool. Hold the chunk in both hands, and extend your arms until they're straight out at shoulder level over a nonstick work surface. (Make sure that this surface

▶ **Tip:** A third of a 25-pound (11.3 kg) brick of clay yields a 14 x 22-inch (35.6 x 55.9 cm) slab that's ⅜ inch (1 cm) thick.

is larger than the size that you want to make the slab.) Throw the clay down onto the surface with a semicircular sweep of your arms so that it hits the work surface with enough force to stretch and thin it somewhat. You can control the slab's length and width by turning the piece as you repeat the tossing motion.

If you need a slab that has specific dimensions and an even thickness throughout, keep in mind that the edges of a tossed slab can be thinner. You might want to make the slab larger than required and then cut it to the needed measurements.

Often, you'll need a slab that has a specific thickness. Some ceramists check the width of a tossed slab with a needle tool. Simply insert the tool into the clay, place a thumbnail on the tool where it meets the clay surface, and then pull out the tool with the thumb still in position. Hold the needle tool against a ruler to check the distance from the tip to your thumbnail.

■ ROLLING

This method is ideal when you want to make a slab that's a precise width (but not length), with an even thickness throughout. Using a slab roller is the most efficient way to roll clay, but it isn't the only method. If you don't have a slab roller, you can hand roll. Both methods are described here.

The width of a hand-rolled slab can't exceed the length of the rolling pin.

Hand Rolling

All you need for hand rolling are two lath strips (or narrow pieces of wood that are the exact same thickness) and a rolling pin, dowel rod, or piece of PVC pipe. The width of the strips determines the thickness of the final slab.

Place a slice of clay on the ware board or other nonstick work surface. Position a lath on each side of the clay. The laths need to be far enough apart to give the clay room to spread, but close enough together for the rolling pin ends to rest on them. Run the rolling pin across the top of the clay. Continue to do this so that the clay thins a bit more with each pass. Every few passes, release the clay from the work surface by picking it up with your hands and then returning it to the surface. Once you can move the roller across the laths without meeting any resistance from the clay, the slab is the desired thickness.

Using a Slab Roller

Some slab rollers can't be set to create a slab that's a precise thickness. You solve this problem using a shim, which has a similar function to the wood strips (or laths) employed for hand rolling (see page 24 for instructions to make a set of shims). The shim sets the roller bars the proper distance apart to make the slab the desired thickness. Let's say you want to make a slab that's ³⁄₈ inch (1 cm) thick. Place a shim of this width between the roller bars, and then raise or lower the rollers until the shim fits snugly between them. **1**

Run one piece of canvas through the roller bars until a little of it shows on the opposite side.

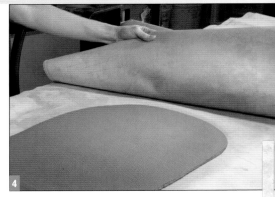

Center a slice of clay, very near the roller bars, on that canvas sheet. **2** Drape a second sheet of canvas over the clay, with the leading edge close to the rollers.

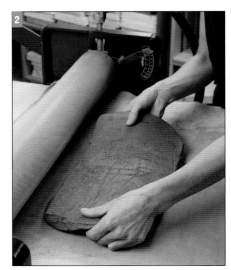

Turn the roller's rotary handle clockwise, at the same time pushing the clay until the roller bars grab it. **3** Continue cranking the handle until the clay slab has emerged from the other side. Expect the width to increase only by a couple of inches (about 5 cm).

Remove the top layer of canvas. **4** Refer to the next section to learn how to shift the clay onto a ware board.

■ MOVING A SLAB

Select a ware board that's larger than the slab, and place it next to the slab. Grasp the leading edge of the canvas, and tug on it to pull the slab onto the ware board. Keep the slab as flat as possible while transferring it onto the ware board. This is important because clay has memory: If you curve it during the move it may revert back to the curved shape during the drying or firing process.

Use a large rib to smooth the clay's surface. **5** Lay another ware board that's the same size as the first one on top of the slab. Hold both ware boards together, and flip them over. Remove the top ware board and canvas to reveal a perfectly flat slab.

Project: **Footed Bowl**

It won't take long for you to develop a feel for shaping an attractive, well-balanced bowl. In the meantime, count on the simple process explained here to create a thing of beauty. The secret to success is using a bowl you already own—or a slump mold—to shape your soft clay slab.

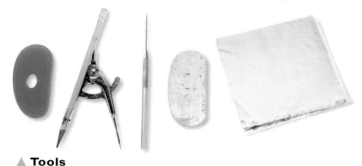

▲ **Tools**

Soft rubber rib, compass, needle tool, metal serrated rib, canvas cloth

1 Look for a kitchen bowl with an appealing shape if you don't have an appropriate slump mold. The bowl doesn't have to have a smooth interior but keep in mind that any texture will transfer onto the clay. Avoid using a bowl with a pronounced lip. Place the bowl (or the slump mold) on a ware board. If your chosen bowl is glass, metal, glazed clay, or other nonporous material, cover it with a thin plastic sheet. Place a tape measure flat inside the form. Measure the length and width from edge to edge.

RELATED TECHNIQUES

Molds	Remoistening Clay	Moving a Slab
21	**11**	**48**

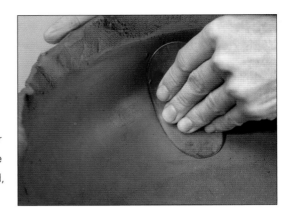

2 Roll a slab ⅜ inch (1 cm) thick that's wider and longer than the bowl measurement. The slab needs to be resting on a canvas sheet. Use the needle tool to cut the slab to the shape of the mold, using the step 1 measurement plus 4 inches (10.2 cm) for an overhang. Cradle the canvas and slab with your forearms. Lay the slab, canvas side up, over the center of the mold so that it drapes into the interior. Pull off the canvas. Slide the soft rubber rib along the exposed clay surface to press it against the mold, smooth out any wrinkles, and then return the slab to an even thickness.

▶ **Tip:** A ⅜-inch-thick (1 cm) slab is good for a bowl that has an 8-inch diameter (20.3 cm) and is 5 inches (12.7 cm) deep.

3 Patch any parts of the slab that may have thinned (see page 26). Rest the needle tool on the rim of the mold at a 90° angle. Hold the clay against the inside of the mold, and slide the needle tool inward until it pierces through the clay. Glide the needle tool around the perimeter of the bowl, along the rim, until all the excess clay has been trimmed off. Save the scrap pieces of clay under a thin plastic sheet for use in step 5.

4 Let the slab dry in the mold until it's leather hard. Place a ware board on top of the mold. Hold the ware board and the mold together and flip them upside down. The clay form will release onto the ware board so that you can remove the mold. Set the compass to half the desired diameter of the bowl's foot. Center the compass on the bottom of the bowl and lightly sketch a circle. Measure the circle's circumference with the measuring tape.

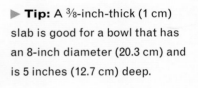

5 Combine the moist clay scraps into a ⅜-inch-thick (1 cm) slab that can be cut to a width proportionate to the bowl's size and the same length as the circle's circumference. The width of the strip (which will create the height of the foot) needs to balance the size and shape of the bowl. Experiment with the dimensions. Place the strip on the bottom of the bowl, shaping it to the scored circle. Maintaining this shape, place the strip on the ware board. You may need to join more than one strip to complete the circumference of the scored circle.

6 Score one lengthwise edge of the foot and on the drawn circle on the bottom of the bowl, using the metal serrated rib. Run a line of slip along the scored clay with a slip applicator, and press the pieces together. Wipe off any excess slip. Roll two thin coils. Apply one to the inside seam, where the foot meets the bottom of the bowl, and another to the outside seam. Blend the coils to reinforce the seam.

7 Turn the bowl right side up. The rim is an intrinsic part of the function of a bowl. It should be smooth and inviting, not coarse or sharp-edged. Slide a damp chamois cloth around the rim to refine the edge. Place the bowl on the banding wheel or lazy Susan, and give it a 360° turn to assess the bowl's balance and composition. Make any adjustments, remoistening the piece, if needed. Decorate and fire the piece as desired. The finished bowl shown on page 49 was painted with a generous application of white slip while leather hard. The rim and foot were decorated and, once bisqued, the bowl was coated with a golden transparent glaze and then refired.

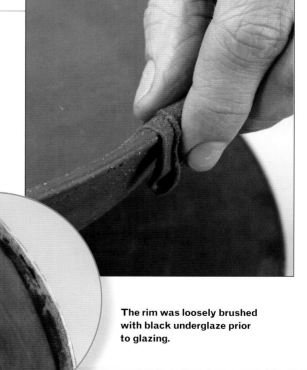

The rim was loosely brushed with black underglaze prior to glazing.

Project: **Wall Pocket**

A hump mold can help you form a clay slab to a specific shape. This process is much simpler than you might expect because a soft-clay slab is so flexible. The only challenge is dealing with areas where portions of the slab overlap. The solution is presented in the steps for this project.

▶ **Tools**

Needle tool, scoring tool, rigid rubber rib, round-edged wood modeling tool, hole maker, metal serrated rib

1 Measure the width of the hump mold from edge to edge and calculate half that length. Add 2 inches (5.1 cm) to both the width and length. Roll out a ¼-inch-thick (6 mm) slab that's twice this size. Use the needle tool to cut the slab in half. One half is for the front (or face) of the pocket, and the remaining piece is for the back. For the time being, set aside the back piece. Spritz it with water, if necessary, and cover it with a thin plastic sheet to keep it moist until you're ready to work on it.

▶ **Tip:** You also need an oval slump mold (or suitable alternative) to make this bowl.

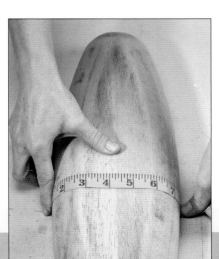

The wooden mold used for the finished wall pocket shown here measures 9 x 21 x 2 inches (22.9 x 53.3 x 5.1 cm).

RELATED TECHNIQUES

Molds	Moving a Slab	Stamp Appliqué
21	**48**	**71**

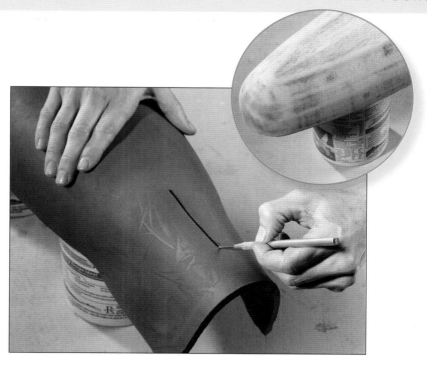

2 Elevate the mold with *coddles* (two soup cans are suitable) to give you access to the underside. Drape the clay shape for the pocket's face over the mold. Use your hands to push the clay flat against the sides of the mold. Make a lengthwise cut with the needle tool a couple of inches from the end of the mold to the end of the clay.

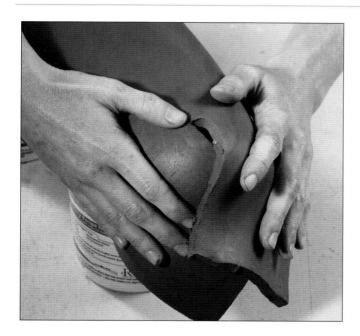

3 Fold one end of the cut side of the clay over the other. Press the edges of the overlapped clay flush against the mold. Cut through both layers of the clay at the bottom of the mold. Gently reach under the cut edges and pull out the extra layer of clay that's closest to the mold on both sides of the cut edge.

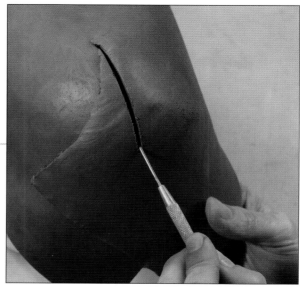

4 Rough up both sides of the cut edge with a scoring tool. Use the slip applicator to apply slip to one edge. Press the cut edges together and then wipe off the excess slip. Press a ⅜-inch-diameter (9.5 mm) coil to the outside of the seam, and then stroke it to smooth and blend (fuse) it into the surface.

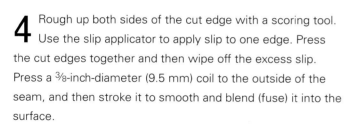

5 Cut off the excess clay around the edges of the mold. Measure from the bottom of the form up to the desired position for the wall pocket's rim. Make two marks with a needle tool, about 2 inches (5.1 cm) apart for the rim. Align one long side of a flexible straightedge with the marks and across the form. Use this edge as your guide to cut the rim with the needle tool.

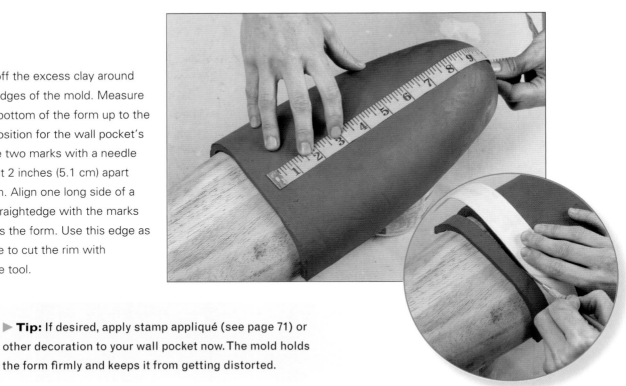

▶ **Tip:** If desired, apply stamp appliqué (see page 71) or other decoration to your wall pocket now. The mold holds the form firmly and keeps it from getting distorted.

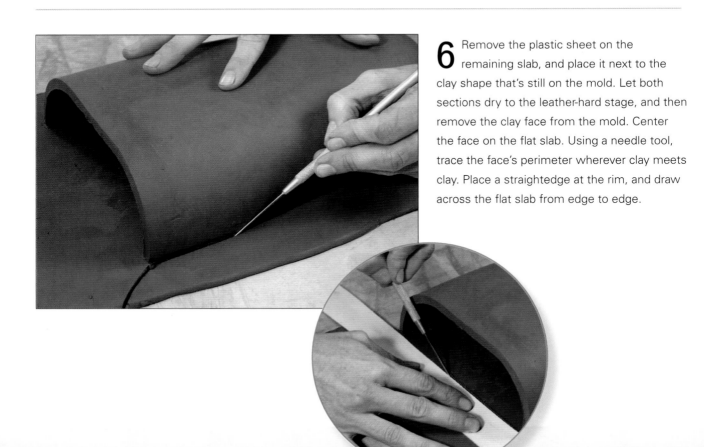

6 Remove the plastic sheet on the remaining slab, and place it next to the clay shape that's still on the mold. Let both sections dry to the leather-hard stage, and then remove the clay face from the mold. Center the face on the flat slab. Using a needle tool, trace the face's perimeter wherever clay meets clay. Place a straightedge at the rim, and draw across the flat slab from edge to edge.

7 Lift off the face and cut through the slab along the drawn lines. Set aside the excess slab under a thin plastic sheet. Keep the back on the ware board so that it stays flat. Score the back and the face where the shapes will meet. Add slip to the scored area on the bottom, and press the two shapes together. Reinforce this seam on both the inside and outside with a coil, blending the outside coil with a rigid rubber rib and using the round-edged wooden tool to smooth the coil placed along the inside of the seam.

▶ **Tip:** You can attach a moist clay coil to a stiff or leather-hard piece despite their different stages of dryness, as long as the area to be reinforced is small and the coil is thoroughly fused to the form.

8 Once the seam is fused and strong, carefully lift the piece from the ware board. Place it facedown on a soft surface so that you can access the back without distorting the form. Use a hole maker or needle tool to cut a ⅜-inch-diameter (9.5 mm) hole in the center of the back, 1½ inches (3.8 cm) from the top. This hole accommodates a screw for hanging the finished piece. Place the piece faceup on the ware board to help the back dry flat.

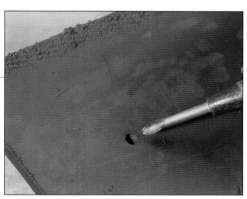

9 Cut out a rectangle of clay to the depth of the face's opening at the center. Let this *bridge* dry to the leather-hard stage. Taper one of the long edges. This bridge supports the face while it dries. Make sure the clay bridge is at the same level of dryness; it must dry at the same rate as the wall pocket so they will shrink together. Remove the bridge once the piece is bone dry. Consider how you're going to use the wall pocket: If it will be used to hold a flower arrangement, the interior should be glazed so it can hold water.

Stamp appliqué can add beautiful definition to the rim without distracting attention from the overall form. Choose a design that's appropriate for the size of the form.

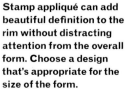

Slab-Built Gallery

Fran Welch
Redflower Dream, 2007

15 x 6 x 3½ inches (38.1 x 15.2 x 8.9 cm)
Slab, pinched, and coiled white earthenware and Clague's Clay
sculptural body; high-temp wire and nails, metal found objects; underglaze, Mason stains; electric fired; encaustic and oils, post-fire
Photo by Steve Mann

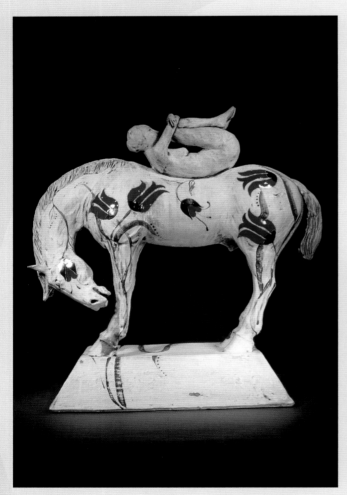

Sue Tirrell
Persian Rider, 2004

21 x 21x 10 inches (53.3 x 53.3 x 25.4 cm)
Slab-built earthenware; electric fired, cone 04;
slip, terra sigillata, glazes, underglazes, luster
Photo by artist

Sandi Pierantozzi
Salt & Pepper Set, 2006

5 x 7 x 3 inches (12.7 x 17.8 x 7.6 cm)
Slab-built porcelain; satin glaze; electric fired
Photo by artist

Liz Zlot Summerfield
Creamer and Sugar Set, 2007

3 x 6 x 2½ inches (7.6 x 15.2 x 6.4 cm)
Hand-built earthenware; terra sigillata, glaze, under-glaze luster; electric fired
Photo by artist

Sandi Pierantozzi
Canister Set, 2006

Largest, 6 x 5 x 4 inches (15.2 x 12.7 x 10.2 cm)
Slab-built porcelain; satin glaze; electric fired
Photo by artist

Aaron Calvert
Ray Stone, 2003

4 x 6 x 2 inches (10.2 x 15.2 x 5.1 cm)
Slab-constructed earthenware; glazes, enamel; electric fired
Photo by artist

Technique: **Slab Building**

Slab construction is all about joining the shapes to make boxes and other rigid, predominantly geometric, forms. A common way of working with soft slabs is draping them over a form until the clay is firm. The construction of stiff slab forms, on the other hand, begins with flat shapes that are cut from clay, dried slightly, and then assembled like pieces of wood.

Cut out shapes from the slabs using templates and a needle tool. **1** Carefully pull away any scrap pieces of the slab. Only the shapes remain on the ware board. Sandwich the shapes between two drywall ware boards until the clay reaches the stiff stage. The ware boards prevent the shapes from warping while they dry.

Stiff and leather-hard clay pieces can't be fused together with your fingers and thumb, as you do with moist clay. Instead, you seam the pieces by scoring the clay  and applying a slip to essentially glue the pieces together. If you have trouble scoring along the edge of a shape, slide it to the edge of the ware board for better accessibility. Any shapes not being used should be stored under a thin plastic sheet to retain the moisture content.

Edges that will be joined to make a 90° angle first need to be cut at a 45° angle. This is easy with a mitering tool: Just start the tool at one end of an edge and drag it along the length of the edge. **2** The wire will cut a perfect angle. Save the remnants from the mitered edges—with the angles and lengths intact—under a thin plastic sheet to keep them at their current stage of dryness. You will use them later to reinforce the seams.

Apply slip to the scored surfaces with a paintbrush or slip applicator. **4** To attach two prepared shapes, bring the bottom edge of a wall toward the form's base shape at a 45° angle. It's a good idea to let the base rest on a banding wheel or lazy Susan during assembly. This lets you turn the work without touching the form more than necessary. (Handling shapes as little as possible ensures they stay straight.) Now raise the wall to its final, vertical position. All vertical sections should be joined to the base in this way, touching first the base and then an adjoining wall. Don't wipe off the excess slip inside the joined corner.

Before adding the last wall, reinforce each joined edge, or seam, with the mitered scraps you set aside earlier. Press the scrap to the interior of the corner. The 90° angle of the mitered scrap fits perfectly into the seam. Stroke the attached scrap with your fingertip or the rubber rib tool to smooth the seam. **5**

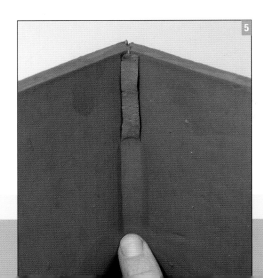

Project: **Geometric Vessel**

Stiff slab construction is similar to working with flexible pieces of wood. Both are rigid, but the clay can still be manipulated, if needed. You'll begin to understand this characteristic of stiff slabs when you handle and join the shapes for this vessel. At the same time, this project shows you how to construct an elegant form.

▲ **Tools**

Metal ruler, needle tool, mitering tool, wood-handle scoring tool, rigid rubber rib, paddle

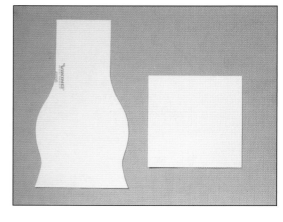

1 Make the Wall and Base templates from card stock.

RELATED TECHNIQUES

2 Roll a slab ¼ inch (6 mm) thick that measures 28 x 18 inches (71.1 x 45.7 cm). Position it on a ware board. Cut out four Walls and a Base from the moist slab using the needle tool. Sandwich the shapes between two ware boards and let them dry to a stiff stage. Try not to bend the shapes if you handle them.

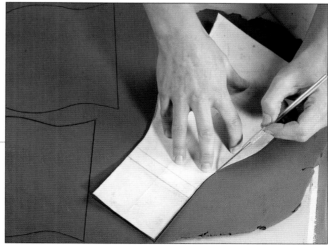

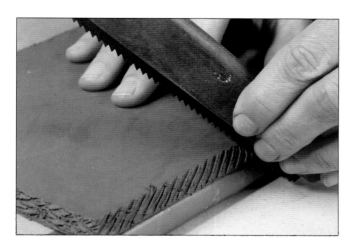

3 Miter all four sides of the Base, as well as the sides and bottom edges of the Walls at 45° angles. Leave the top edges of the Walls square. Save the remnants from the mitered edges for use in a later step. Score the mitered angles with a scoring tool.

▶ **Tip:** Handle these stiff slab shapes as little as possible to ensure that they stay straight.

4 Place the Base on a small ware board and then place both on a banding wheel or lazy Susan, if available. Use the slip applicator to apply a small amount of slip to the scored edges of the Base. Using too much slip could create excessive moisture and weaken the structure of the piece. Apply slip to the scored edges of one of the Walls. Holding this Wall at a 45° angle, bring its bottom edge toward the Base to meet one of its mitered edges.

5 Lift the Wall into its final vertical position. Apply slip to the mitered edges of another Wall shape, and place it against the Base at an edge adjacent to the one with the attached Wall. Tip the new Wall up, allowing the vertical edge to touch the adjoining Wall. All Wall sections should be joined to the Base this way. Wipe any excess slip off the exterior of the form, but let slip ooze out of the inside of the seams.

6 Before attaching the last Wall, push the entire length of a mitered scrap into one of the corners of the developing form. The 90° angle of the mitered scrap fits perfectly into the seam. Reinforce the other corner the same way. Attach the back Wall with slip and also reinforce the remaining corners with the mitered scraps.

7 Turning the structure as you go, paddle the Walls to make any necessary adjustments to the shape. Strike the outside of the seam while bracing the inside with your hand. Paddling allows you to adjust the shape of a form, reinforce seams, and square up the edges.

8 Smooth the surfaces with your fingers and a rigid rubber rib. Soften the rim with a moist chamois cloth. The finished vessel shown on page 60 was painted with white slip. The design was applied with a slip trailing applicator and then fired.

After it was bisque fired, the entire form was dipped in a green transparent glaze and then fired again.

Project: **Carved Lantern**

A lantern creates a beautiful ambience for both indoor and outdoor settings. You can enhance the effect created by the candlelight placed inside the form by cutting shapes out of the walls during the building process. The instructions for this lantern include guidance to make a fitted, removable lid.

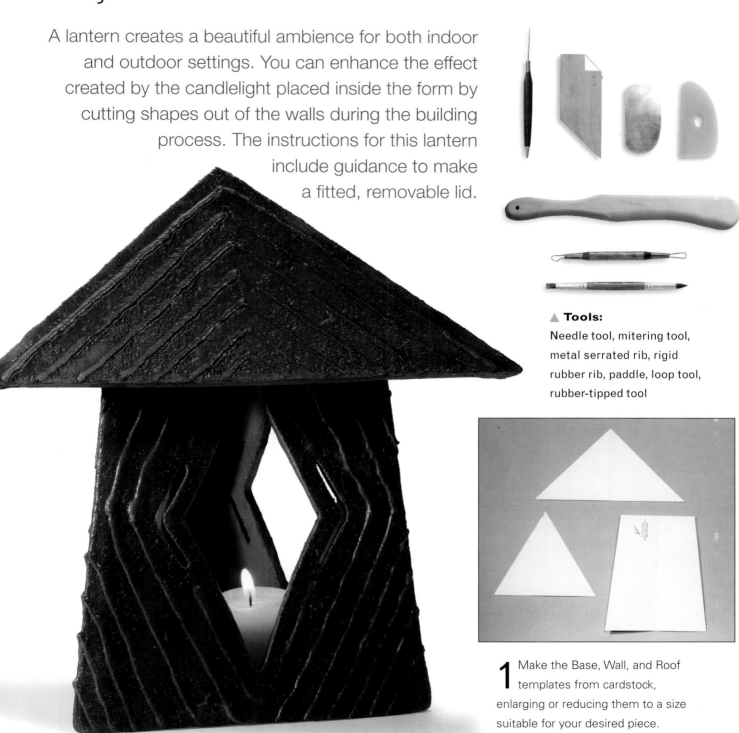

▲ Tools:
Needle tool, mitering tool, metal serrated rib, rigid rubber rib, paddle, loop tool, rubber-tipped tool

1 Make the Base, Wall, and Roof templates from cardstock, enlarging or reducing them to a size suitable for your desired piece.

2 Roll a slab ¼ inch (6 mm) thick and large enough to accommodate the size of the templates. This slab will be thinner so that the negative shapes will be easier to cut. Place the templates on the slab, and use the needle tool to cut out the shapes. You need three Walls, one Base, and three Roof shapes.

> ▶ **Tip:** You may need more than one slab if you substantially increase the size of the templates to make a large lantern.

3 Sandwich the sections between two ware boards until they dry to the leather-hard stage. Miter all the edges of the Base with 45° angles. Miter the side and bottom edges of the Walls as well (leave the top edges square). Miter the sides of the Roof shapes (leave the bottom edges square). Save the remnants from the mitered edges for use in a later step.

4 Score all the mitered edges with a serrated rib. Cover the Roof shapes with a thin plastic sheet, and set them aside. Place the Base on a bat or small ware board, and set them both on a banding wheel. Use the slip applicator to apply slip to all the scored edges of the Base and Walls. Attach two Walls to the Base and to each other, as described in steps 3 and 4 of the Geometric Vessel project (see page 60).

5 Before attaching the final Wall, reinforce all of the seams with the mitered scraps saved in step 2. Square up the angles of the joined Walls by tapping them with the paddle, while using your hand to brace the opposite side of the form. Smooth the surface even more with your fingers or the rigid rubber rib, if needed. While still on the bat or ware board, cover the piece with a thin plastic sheet to keep it moist, and set it aside.

6 Apply slip to the scored edges of the Roof shapes. Leave one shape flat on a ware board and attach a Roof shape to each side, reinforcing the seams with the mitered scraps as you do the assembly. Once the two sections are attached, apply the remaining section and reinforce this last seam. Place the Roof on the ware board, and adjust the angles with a paddle, if needed. Smooth the surface and edges with the rigid rubber rib, if needed.

7 Take the plastic off the assembled Base and Walls, and place the assembled roof on top of the form. Give the form a 360° turn to make sure the roof is on straight. Use the needle tool to mark inside each corner of the roof where the roof meets the tops of the Walls. The mark is for a flange, which is a small attachment that stabilizes the roof's position on the Walls.

8 Remove the roof, and measure up 1 1/2 inches (3.8 cm) from the mark, toward the pointed top. Mark this new position in all three corners. You're going to place the finished flange just above this mark. Roll a coil 4 inches (10.2 cm) long with a 1/8-inch (3 mm) diameter, and form it into a spiral. Pinch the spiral into a triangle. Make two more triangular flanges so you have one for each corner. Let them dry to the stiff stage.

9 Use the serrated rib to score one flat side of each flange and the areas inside the roof where they'll be attached. Add a small amount of slip to the scored areas on the flanges. Press the flanges on the roof. Place the roof back on the form, making sure the flanges hold it evenly on top of the Walls. If necessary, shift the position of one or all of the flanges.

10 Evenly remoisten both the roof and the lantern when they fit perfectly together. Now wait until they reach the stiff-slab stage in about an hour, depending on the relative humidity in your studio. Once the clay is remoistened, use the needle tool to draw a design for the negative spaces on the exterior of the Walls. Using the loop and needle tools and starting at the corners, cut out the shapes. Make several strokes along each design line, until you have cut completely through the clay Wall.

11 Let the piece dry to the leather-hard stage after you cut out all of the shapes. With the lid still in place, clean up and smooth the exterior cut edges with a rubber-tipped tool. Remove the lid once the piece is nearly bone dry, and clean the inside of the lantern before bisque firing. Glaze the inside of the lantern where the candle will sit. If any candle wax spills, it'll be easier to remove from a glazed surface. As with any lidded form, fire the lantern with the lid in place so that the sections shrink together. This will insure a perfect fit.

▶ **Tip:** Bring an outdoor lantern inside when temperatures are below freezing. Atmospheric moisture that's trapped in a porous clay body will expand as the piece freezes and may crack the clay.

A stonelike matte glaze accents the slip-trailed design of the finished lantern.

Slab-Built Gallery

Chris Theiss
Dummy, 2006

Slab-built earthenware; sgraffito,
vitreous slip; electric fired
Photo by artist

Tae-Hoon Kim
Picnic Outward into Space, 2007

34 x 18 x 7 inches (86.4 x 45.7 x 17.8 cm)
Hand-built stoneware and porcelain; glaze; gas fired
Photo by artist

Myung-Jin Kim
Birdcage Jar, 2007

18 x 12½ x 12½ inches (45.7 x 31.8 x 31.8 cm)
Hand-built porcelain; underglaze, clear glaze
Photo by Tony Cunha

Technique: **Making and Using Stamps**

Stamps allow anyone—of any skill level—to develop the most creative surface designs. Stamping is incredibly easy because moist clay readily accepts the impression of any texture. Whatever your aesthetic, you're bound to find or create a stamp with texture or a motif that wlll suit the form you want to make.

THIS SECTION EXPLAINS suitable qualities for a found-object stamp, how to make several types of stamps, and describes the stamp appliqué process.

IF YOU'RE FEELING ADVENTUROUS, go on a treasure hunt for objects that can be used as stamps. You can find texture in nature as subtle as tree bark or as distinct as a leaf or seashell. Look for potential stamps in jewelry, mechanical parts, or even a carved architectural detail. Once you start looking, you'll see texture on objects you've never noticed before.

Recessed or carved areas in the finished stamp will make raised areas in the clay surface. If an object has a porous surface, such as unfinished wood, unglazed clay, or plaster, you can impress it directly into clay. If an object has a surface that's metal, plastic, glass, glazed clay, or other nonporous material, the clay might stick to that material. You can still use these objects if you brush a light dusting of cornstarch, which acts as a resist medium, on the stamp's surface. (Cornstarch residue burns out during the firing process.) Whatever you decide to use, just make sure that the surface doesn't have any undercuts (see page 21).

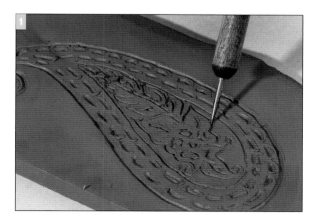

BISQUE STAMPS

Making stamps is a great way to utilize the scraps of clay that remain when you cut a shape from a slab that's at least $3/8$ inch (1 cm) thick.

For a one-of-a-kind stamp, simply draw a freehand design directly onto the scrap. Use a needle tool for incising the lines in the clay. Another option is to transfer an existing drawing or copyright-free image. First, lay it over the clay. Then use a ball stylus to trace over the design lines, applying enough pressure to leave impressions in the clay.

Letters in a design need to be drawn backwards in the clay. This is easier if you make a paper pattern that can be placed on top of the clay and then traced. Start by using a black marker to write as you normally would on a piece of paper. Place the paper, wrong side up, on the clay to see the backward letters that you incise in the clay.

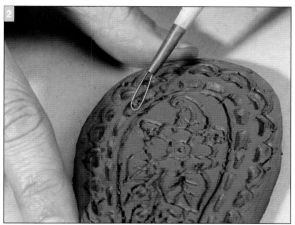

To finish the stamp, you'll need a needle tool, carving tools, a scoring tool, and slip. Draw the image into the clay with a ball stylus, **1** and then accentuate the tracing by cutting out bits of clay with the loop and other carving tools. **2** Choose tools that make wider and deeper lines than you want for the finished piece, to compensate for the shrinkage that happens as the clay stamp dries and is fired. Vary the depth or width of your carving to make interesting designs or textures.

Cut another slab scrap that's slightly larger than the etched piece. Let both dry until they're leather hard. Score the back of the etched shape and one side of the plain scrap. Apply slip onto the scored surface of the stamp, **3** and press them together. The plain backer slab gives the stamp additional strength. After bisque firing, all that tedious work will pay off with dozens of identical stamped impressions.

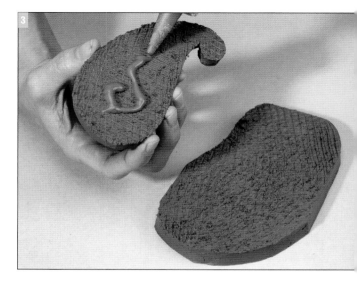

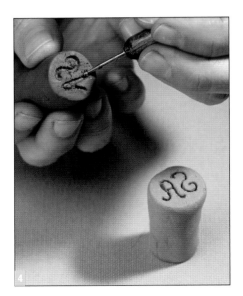

CHOP MARK

A stamp can help you leave a unique and permanent mark, like a painter's signature, on every piece that you make. This personal identification is called a chop mark. You incise initials or a small symbol into a wad of clay that was rolled into a short, thick coil with a diameter that's wide enough to accommodate the mark.

Cut the clay wad to 3 inches (7.6 cm) long so it's comfortable to hold. Make one end smooth and even, to accept your mark. Make this mark a bit larger than desired to allow for shrinkage during drying. **4** If the carving tool leaves a crumbly residue, or burr, wait until the piece is bone dry before brushing it off. Bisque fire the stamp, and it'll be ready to use.

HOT-GLUE STAMP

Once a trail of hot glue has dried on a wood surface, you can use the piece to leave beautiful impressions in clay. All you need is a hot-glue gun and one or more glue sticks, a scrap of wood with one flat surface, some sandpaper, and a permanent felt marker.

Wipe off any dust on the wood scrap, scuff the flat surface with the sandpaper, and then draw your design on the surface with the marker. **5**

Trace over the drawing with a trail of glue from the hot-glue gun. **6** Be very careful; the hot glue and the gun tip are extremely hot. (Keep a small bowl of water nearby so that you can douse a finger if hot glue lands on it.) Achieve additional interesting texture with tendril-like strings that are left when you release the trigger and draw the glue gun away from the stamp. The hot glue dries as soon as it has cooled off. At this point you're ready to stamp with it.

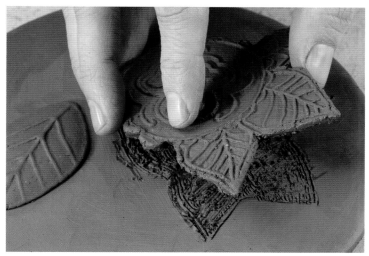

Always score the area where you will apply the stamp appliqué.

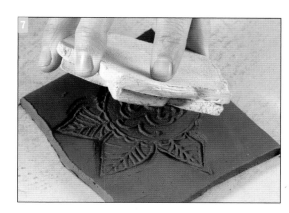

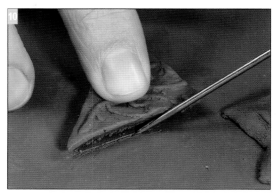

▓ STAMP APPLIQUÉ

You can apply a stamp to a moist clay slab, cut the stamped image from the slab, and then apply this shape to your form. This is called a stamp appliqué.

For this process, gather your stamp, needle tool, and serrated rib or wire scoring tools, and some slip.

It's best to make the appliqué with thin slab scraps; ⅛ inch (3 mm) is suitable. Once you've made all the stamp impressions, **7** cut around the stamps to create interesting shapes. Bevel the edges with a needle tool to give them a tapered look. **8** If you're concerned about distorting the impressed design, harden it by lightly heating the surface with a heat gun or hair dryer. This will preserve the detail of the stamped design.

Now arrange the appliqué pieces on the form. Use a metal rib to shave down the appliqués if they're too thick. **9** When you're happy with the composition, lightly mark their placement on the form with a needle tool. **10** Make sure that all the pieces are the same level of dryness. Remoisten, if necessary (see page 11).

If the appliqué and form are at the leather-hard stage, score the matched surfaces and apply a small amount of slip to the scored area of the stamp appliqué. If you're working with large appliqué pieces, press from the center out to remove any air pockets.

If excess slip oozes out, remove it with a pointed edge of a rubber-tipped tool. Press down all of the edges to hide them and give the appliqué a more refined look.

Project: **Appliqué Tile**

A simple, flat tile is a perfect surface for experimenting with stamps. The most challenging part of this process is keeping the tile flat. Use a clay body that contains a large amount of grog. A clay of this consistency goes a long way toward eliminating warping.

▶ **Tools**

Needle tool, flat-end loop tool, rigid rubber rib, wire scoring tool, metal serrated rib, point-edged rubber-tipped tool

1 Make a stamp for the surface decoration on this piece. Cut a 5 x 8-inch (12.7 x 20.3 cm) template from card stock. Roll a slab ⅜ inch thick (1 cm) and large enough for the number of tiles you want to make. While the slab is moist and still on the ware board, use the template and needle tool to cut one or more tile shapes from the slab. Set aside the scraps under a thin plastic sheet to keep them moist.

▶ **Tip:** A thick tile is less likely to warp during drying and firing.

▶ **Tip:** If your tiles need to be a specific finished size, use a clay ruler (see page 12) to calculate the shrinkage rate of your clay body.

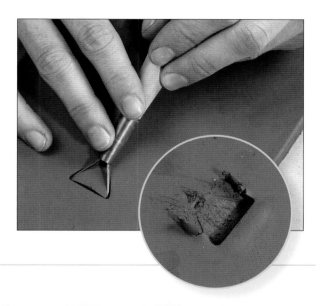

2 Measure 2 inches (5.1 cm) down from the top edge. With the tile's bottom edge closest to you, start pressing down into the clay with the flat-end loop tool. When you're halfway through the depth of the tile, push the tool forward toward the opposite edge of the tile. Slowly ease the tool out of the tile, at the same time pulling out the excess clay.

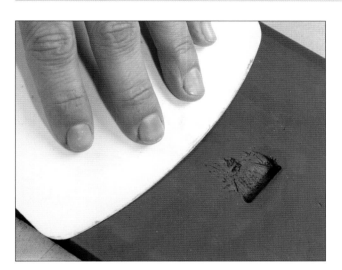

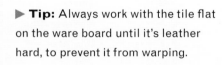

▶ **Tip:** Always work with the tile flat on the ware board until it's leather hard, to prevent it from warping.

3 Swipe the large rubber rib across the recess to remove any raised areas of displaced clay to make the back of the tile flat. While the clay is still moist, smooth the outer edges with your fingers or a soft rib tool. Use a second ware board to flip the tile right side up. Refine the front edges. Cover the tile with a thin plastic sheet, and set it aside for the time being.

4 Toss the slab scraps until they're ⅛ inch (3 mm) thick. Stamp the surface and then cut out some shapes, to make stamp appliqués that you'll apply to the surface of the tile. Take the plastic off the tile and arrange the appliqué pieces on it. Lightly mark their placement on the tile with the needle tool.

5 If necessary, remoisten the tile or stamp appliqués so that all of the pieces are at the same stage of dryness (either stiff or leather hard). Use a wire scoring tool to score the back of the appliqués and the front of the tile at the places they'll be matched. Brush a small amount of slip on the back of each appliqué, and place it on the tile. If you're working with large appliqués, use your fingers to press from the center out to remove any air pockets. Take care not to damage the imprint on the surface.

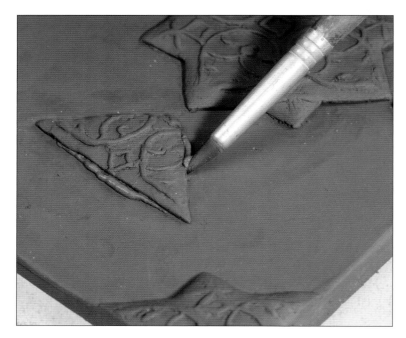

6 If excess slip oozes out, remove it with a point-edged rubber-tipped tool. With your fingertips, press down to hide the cut edges and give the appliqué a refined appearance. Leave the tile flat on the ware board until it's bone dry.

A semiopaque, low-fire cobalt blue glaze looks especially good on a red clay body because the glaze pools in the recessed areas and thins on the raised areas, highlighting the textured design on the stamp appliqué.

Project: **Bird Sculpture**

The trick for creating successful sculpted pieces that won't collapse during forming or firing is using newspaper armatures. These act as temporary supports when sculpting. They remain encased in the clay while you work, and burn out later during the firing process.

◀ **Tools**
Newspaper, masking tape, needle tool, metal serrated rib, soft rubber-tipped tool

RELATED TECHNIQUES

Making and Using Templates	Making Slabs	Stamp Appliqué
23	**46**	**71**

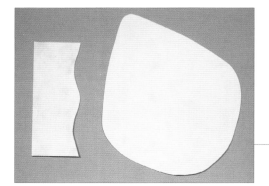

1 Make or buy one or more stamps for the wings and tail feathers. Make the Body and Base templates from cardstock, enlarging or reducing them to a size suitable for your desired piece. Roll a slab to a thickness of ¼ inch (6 mm) and a length and width that will accommodate the templates. Cut one Body and one Base from the clay slab. Store the clay shapes and scraps under a thin plastic sheet until you're ready to use them.

2 Crumple a sheet of newspaper repeatedly to relax the fibers. Smooth out the sheet, and roll it into a narrow oval with tapered ends. Make the diameter no more than half the Body's width and three-quarters of the Body's length. Tape the edges to prevent the shape from unrolling. This is the armature.

▶ **Tip:** Make armatures from soft newspaper so that the crumpled texture won't gouge the clay that's applied.

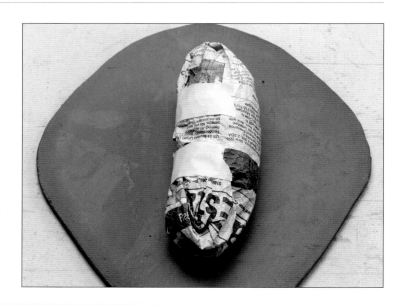

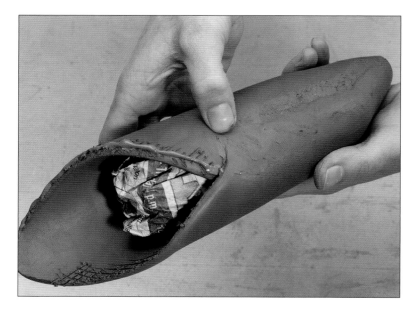

3 Place the armature on the Body, closer to the fat end (the bird's neck). Wrap the Body around the armature to make a cone shape. Mark where the pieces overlap. Open the Body, and score the matching surfaces with the serrated rib. Apply slip to the scored areas, and press them together. Stroke the edges until they're fused. Continue joining the edges until the clay totally encases the newspaper. If necessary, stroke the ends until both are pointed. The thickest part of the shape is closer to one end. Let the Body dry to the stiff-clay stage.

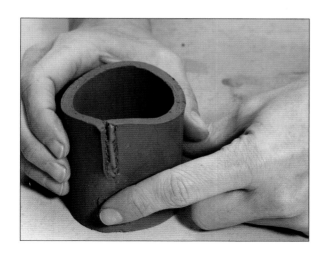

▶ **Tip:** Place drying sculpted shapes on a soft surface, such as a sheet of foam, to prevent the moist clay from sagging and instead conforming to the shape of the flat surface it's resting on.

4 Form the Base into a cylinder with overlapped edges. Score the matched edges, and apply slip on the scored areas. Stroke the edges to fuse them together. Let this piece dry to stiff-slab stage.

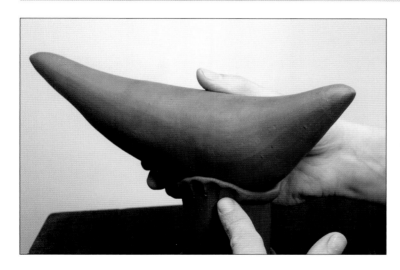

5 Place the Body on the Base. Lightly mark the area on the bird's underside where it will be attached to the Base, using the needle tool. Remove the Body, and score the top of the Base and the Body area just inside the marks. Apply slip to the Base, and fuse the two pieces together. Roll a coil long enough to wrap around the top of the Base and make the diameter ¼ inch (6 mm) thick. While the Base is still moist, drag your index finger vertically through the coil. Add another coil around the bottom of the Base to add stability and decorative continuity.

6 Roll a ball of clay the size of a golf ball. Pinch it into a round bowl to start the head. Leave the bottom ½ inch (1.3 cm) thick. Pinch out the beak with the excess clay at the bottom of the bowl. Elongate the opening to create a neck, and widen it enough to slip over the short, tapered end of the Body. Place the head on the Body. If necessary, cut and taper the opening of the head to ensure a snug fit over the Body.

7 Again place the head on the Body. Lightly mark the area where they overlap, using the needle tool. Remove the head, and score both of the matched areas. Apply slip on the inside of the neck. Place the head over the Body, and gently fuse them together. Use a soft rubber-tipped tool to carve the eyes and other details. Use the needle tool to pierce a small hole in an inconspicuous place to release trapped air inside the Body and head. Air must be able to escape during firing or the form will explode.

8 Toss the clay slab scraps to ⅛ inch (3 mm) thick and stamp them with suitable motifs for tail feathers. Cut out feather shapes from the stamp designs. Experiment with different sizes to find one that appeals to you. Cut the edges at a severe angle using the needle tool. This undercut gives the edges a thinner, more refined appearance. Score and slip the feathers and the Body at the positions the pieces will be joined. Apply the feathers, curving them to the Body. Since these thin appendages can be easily broken off, only extend them 2 or 3 inches (5.1 or 7.6 cm) past the Body.

9 Stamp more of the thin slab scraps for the wings. Cut two free-form wings from the stamped scraps. Finish these stamp appliqués with undercut edges, and apply them to the bird's Body in the same way that you attached the tail feathers.

The finished bird was decorated with underglazes while in the greenware state. A patina solution and decorative glazes were applied for the final firing.

Project: **Nesting Box**

This box project is both sculptural and functional. It's a lidded form with a bird handle on top. This piece is made with leather-hard slabs that are scored and joined with slipped seams. The bird is sculpted with the pinching technique. Stamp appliqués are the finishing touch.

▶ **Tools**
Needle tool, mitering tool, serrated rib tool, pointed rubber-tipped tool, paddle

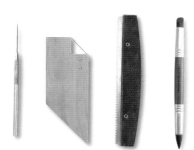

1 Make or buy two rectangular stamps: one should be narrow and the other should be wide (see step 7). You also need a circular medallion stamp. Make the Base, Front and Back Wall, Side Wall, and Roof templates from cardstock, first enlarging or reducing them to a size suitable for your desired piece. Roll a slab ¼ inch (6 mm) thick that's an appropriate length and width for the templates you've made. Place the slab on a large ware board.

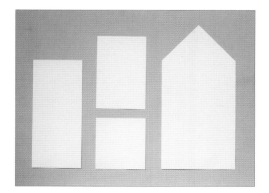

2 Place the templates on the moist slab and cut out the shapes, using the needle tool. You need one Base shape and two of all the rest. Carefully remove the excess clay around the shapes, and store these scraps under a thin plastic sheet to keep them moist for use in step 7. Place another ware board on top of the shapes, and let them dry until they're leather hard. Use the mitering tool to cut all of the edges on the Base, Front and Back Walls, and Roof shapes to a 45° angle. Also cut this angle on all but one upper edge of both of the Side Walls. Store the mitered scraps under a thin plastic sheet.

3 Place a small ware board on a banding wheel, and put the clay Base on top of it. Score all of the edges on the shapes using the serrated rib tool. Attach the bottom of a Front and Back Wall to the Base edge to edge, first applying a small amount of slip on both of the matching, scored edges. Wipe off the excess slip only on the outside of the seams. In the same manner, attach the Side Walls to the Base and first Wall. Press a mitered strip into each corner to reinforce the seams. You don't need to score and slip this scrap.

4 Attach the remaining Front and Back Wall to the developing form, again scoring the edges and using slip in each seam. Reinforce the interior of those remaining seams with more of the scraps. Turn the banding wheel to inspect the entire structure. Trim the top edges if they aren't even and level. Score, apply slip, and then place the Roof sections on the top edges of the Walls.

5 Tap the paddle around the form if the shape needs to be adjusted. Air trapped inside the box will support the form while you're using the paddle on it. Paddling is a great way to reinforce seams because the force compresses the clay particles together. Turn the piece on the banding wheel to inspect all the angles. Continue to make adjustments as needed.

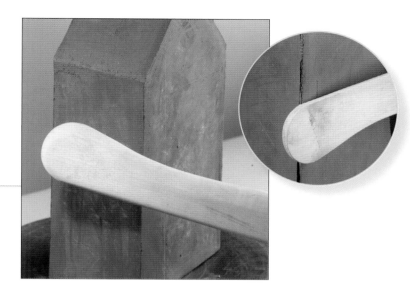

▶ **Tip:** Pieces of a form that should fit together when dry must be kept together as they dry and shrink to ensure a snug fit.

6 Decide where you want to cut the top of the form to make a lid. Using the needle tool, sketch a line around the form. When you draw this line, include a key (a unique shape to indicate the lid's correct orientation on the box). The line is the guide for cutting the lid. Score the line several times, gradually cutting completely through the clay. If the clay is too hard to cut, remoisten it (see page 11). Carefully remove the lid, and reinforce the seams for the roof using scraps that you set aside earlier.

7 Place the lid back on the box. Use the slab scraps set aside in step 2 to make long stamp appliqués for all of the edges. Create these strips in manageable sections, matching their edges so that you have a seamless design when you place them end to end on the box. Make a medallion appliqué. Score the edges of the box and the back of the stamp appliqués, and apply slip on the scored surface of the appliqué pieces. Press the pieces to the box, gently shaping them around the angles. Situate the medallion on the center of the lid.

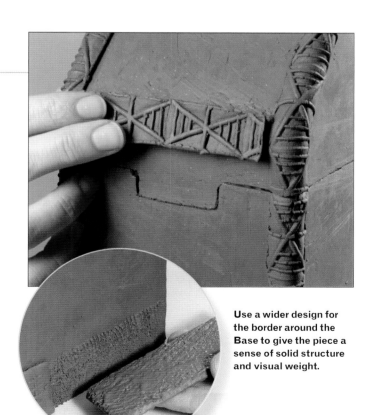

Use a wider design for the border around the Base to give the piece a sense of solid structure and visual weight.

▶ **Tip:** Use stamps that are in proportion to the overall size of the box; decorations should accentuate the form without dominating it.

8 Shape a slab scrap into a wad of clay the size of a small plum. Pinch it into an inverted, elongated, and somewhat fattened triangle. Round off one end to form the head of a bird. At that rounded end, pinch a small cone to form the beak. This is the start of the bird that's positioned on top of the box as a handle.

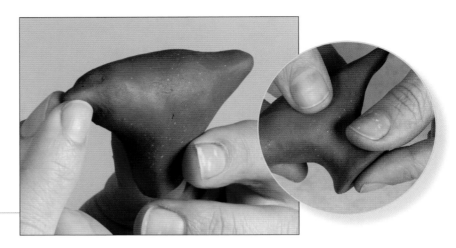

9 Pinch the opposite end to form the tail feathers and then pinch the bottom of the inverted triangle to form a skirt for the Base of the bird form. Make it substantial enough to create a fair amount of surface area for attaching the bird handle to the box. Use the pointed rubber-tip-edged tool to add eyes, feather markings, and other details.

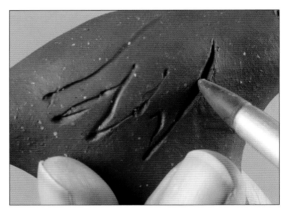

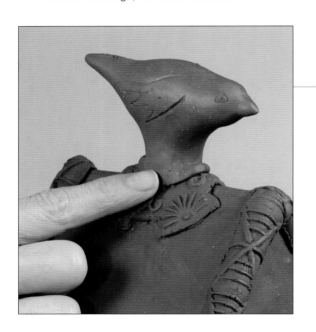

10 When the handle is leather hard, place it on the lid. Use the needle tool to lightly mark the area on the roof where the handle will be attached. Score and slip both areas, and press them together. Reinforce this fused area with a small rolled coil, and blend it smooth. The finished box shown on page 79 was bisque fired, then the entire piece was stained and given a patina with an oxide wash. Then it was fired a second time.

Narrative drawings were inscribed into the featured form when it was leather hard. When the piece was bone dry, the drawings were painted with underglaze.

Stamped Gallery

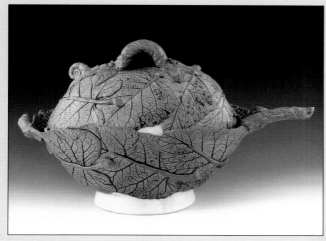

Lynn Fisher
Tureen, 2007

17 x 12 x 11 inches (43.2 x 30.5 x 27.9 cm)
Slab-built stoneware; cone 9-10, oxidation;
impressed burdock leaves
Photo by artist

Barbara Knutson
Oval Pedestal Bowl with Handles, 2001

9 x 7 x 16 inches (22.9 x 17.8 x 40.6 cm)
Slab-built white stoneware; hollow handles; pressed;
rolled dots; bisque cone 06; glaze cone 10 reduction
Photo by Tim Barnwell

Jennifer A. Everett
Tile, 2006

3 x 3 x ⅜ inches (7.6 x 706 x 1 cm)
Extruded stoneware; gas fired in reduction, cone 10;
stamped decoration
Photo by artist

Jonathan Nicklow
Valerie Nicklow
Destination, 2006

8 x 8 x ¾ inches (20.3 x 20.3 x 1.9 cm)
Slab-rolled low-fire white clay; electric fired, cone 04; relief
sculpture, stamped elements, oil paint, tar and varnish
Photo by artist

Rachel Berg
Untitled, 2004

5½ x 4½ x 3 inches (14 x 11.4 x 7.6 cm)
Wheel-thrown and hand-built stoneware; soda
fired, cone 10; impressed designs
Photo by artist

Frank James Fisher
Milk Pitcher, 2005

10½ x 3½ x 6 inches (26.7 x 8.9 x 15.2 cm)
Slab-built porcelain; raku fired
Photo by artist

Kristen Kieffer
Rectangular Tile Forms: Cake, Bijou, and Circlet, 2007

Each, 8 x 5 x 1½ inches (20.3 x 12.7 x 3.8 cm)
Hand-built, slab construction, mid-range porcelain: stamped,
carved, and slip decoration; multiple glazes; electric fired
Photo by artist

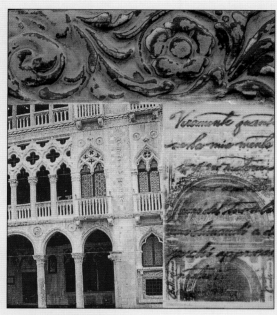

Maggie Mae Beyeler
Ca'd'oro, 2007

6 x 6 x ⁵⁄₁₆ inches (15.2 x 15.2 x 0.8 cm)
Slab-rolled white stoneware; electric fired,
cone 6; laser toner image transfer, cone
04; matte green/bronze glaze, underglaze
stamped text
Photo by Margot Geist

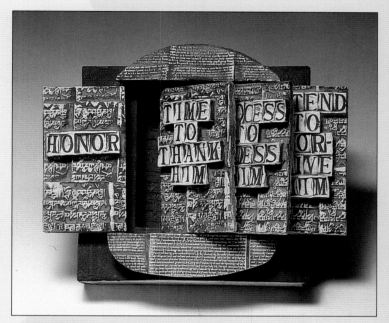

Lana Wilson
Ceramic Book with Moveable Pages, 2003

8 x 10 x 3 inches (20.3 x 25.4 x 7.6 cm)
White stoneware; hand-built slab; stamped, dry
glaze mixtures with two glaze firings; electric fired
Photo by artist

Kathryn Finnerty
Oval Teapot, 2001

6½ x 9 inches (16.5 x 22.9 cm)
Slab construction with raised-line relief; white
slip over terra cotta; cone 04
Photo by Tom Rohr

Inspiration

Discovering a technique and then expressing it in clay is the start of an exciting journey in ceramics. Yet, after absorbing the basics, you may find that you want more…more texture, more color, more than just a basic form. Here's what to do when you reach that point.

IT'S EASY TO ROMANTICIZE CREATIVITY AND INSPIRATION. You find yourself gazing at an amazing piece in a show and think, "Where did that idea come from?" And you don't have to go far to find a ceramist who says of a form or surface decoration, "It just came to me." Some people have a knack for creating innovative hand-built forms, texture, and painterly effects. The results can be magical. But the process isn't. Artists—either consciously or instinctively— learn to use inspiration to tap into their creativity. You can do the same.

■ EXPLORE TECHNIQUES

There's a very old saying that luck is when preparation meets opportunity. The same can be said for creativity: Once you've learned a technique, you can create opportunities that will help you tap into your creativity so that you can develop work that's unique and interesting.

Pick a favorite item, a sunflower for example, and consider ways that you can use a technique to interpret this flower. If you're having trouble getting started, make a list of all the techniques that you enjoy. Now consider how each one can be applied to that item. For a sunflower, you might pinch petal shapes that can be attached to a slab-built form. Or you could pluck a petal, press it into a clay surface, and accentuate the subtle texture with a patina (see page 110).

Clay tiles have a good area for exploring surface applications. Here, they're used to play with glazes and colors that frame and enhance vintage bird decals.

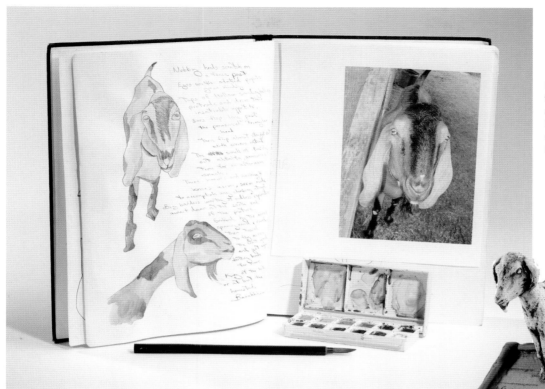

Don't worry about the quality of your drawing. You don't have to focus on creating a beautiful image.

■ START A SKETCHBOOK

When you see an interesting image, cut it out and tape it into a notebook. Better yet, try sketching it. Your goal is to gain an understanding of the shape of the subject, its color or variations in colors, and the surface texture. This knowledge leads to intelligent decisions about types of clay, construction techniques, and surface decoration for a piece based on that subject.

You can see this process of studying a form and then interpreting it in a ceramic form in the sketchbook and clay box. Note how the watercolors in the sketchbook capture the goat's neck extension, the shape of the head, and the position of the eyes. Paying attention to these details and having the sketches to reference led to the whimsical creature on top of the box. (This piece is part of a series that includes the Nesting Box project on page 79. As you work on the projects in this book, consider how you can make them your own.)

▪ FREE ASSOCIATE

Take a bit of time to look around your environment and think about your life. What are your passions? Are you drawn to color or texture? For some people, identifying their favorite textures, colors, and passions is difficult. You may find your answers in an afternoon or over a month or two. You may even need to work with clay for quite some time until, one day, you discover that a trend or theme has been emerging all along.

Developing a piece that expresses a concept you care about isn't always easy, but many have found success with free association. Try putting your concept or idea on paper and then jot down other ideas, words, and images that come to mind. Some ideas translate into a color; red is frequently associated with anger, for example. Some shapes are universal symbols, such as a dove for peace. Other shapes may have symbolism only for you but, once created in clay, the meaning will become apparent to others. Don't stop yourself from writing down a crazy idea that's forming, because it might lead you somewhere interesting. Eventually, an image will emerge. Once you have a tangible form in mind, you can start working with your clay.

A series of self-portraits in clay inevitably led to more pinched pieces that express love for the family pets. These forms were painted with underglaze and slip while in the greenware state. A patina solution was applied at the bisque stage, and then they were fired again.

▪ LOOK BACK

Another way to explore a theme is to take a look at your past works. You may find yourself returning again and again to the same shape or glaze. Now that you're aware of this trend, you can continue to develop it, pushing the application and materials in a different direction with each new form. Your most successful piece could be very different from the earlier ones. To someone outside this process, who sees only the one you like the most, you've created magic.

You can mull over ideas, but inspiration really takes off when you take action. In other words, stop thinking, grab a hunk of clay, and go play!

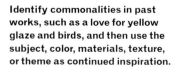

Identify commonalities in past works, such as a love for yellow glaze and birds, and then use the subject, color, materials, texture, or theme as continued inspiration.

Technique: **Surface Decoration**

This section introduces you to materials that can be applied to greenware. Later in this same chapter, you can learn how to use these materials for seven well-known techniques: sgraffito, inlay, slip brushwork, slip trailing, stenciling, burnishing, and painting with underglaze (see pages 90 to 99).

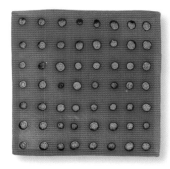

AT ALMOST EVERY STAGE IN CLAY WORK you have the opportunity to enhance a form. You've probably heard about adding glaze to a form when it reaches the greenware stage (see page 11). Yet there are other materials and techniques that you can apply before—or in place of—glazing.

It's easy to become captivated by any of the materials and techniques that are introduced here. If this happens, it won't be hard for you to track down entire books about surface decoration, which can guide your further exploration.

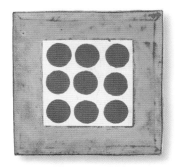

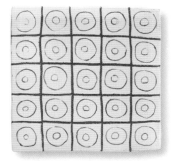

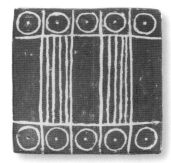

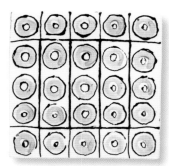

Expand your repertoire with, top to bottom, burnishing, stenciling, sgraffito, underglaze painting, inlay, slip trailing, and slip brushwork.

■ MATERIALS

Slip, engobe, terra sigillata, and underglaze, which are all explained in this section, are kind of like a ceramist's paint box. When used with one or more classic surface treatment techniques, they can give your piece a unique look and feel. Before you start using any of these materials, it's a good idea to develop a basic understanding of them, so you can choose the one that can best enhance your piece.

Slip and engobe recipes begin with a white base, to which colorants, such as natural oxides or manufactured Mason stains, are added.

SLIPS AND ENGOBES are, essentially, thinned down clay. You use one or the other to color a piece, add texture, or act as a ground for a decorative technique. Engobes, which contain less clay than slip, can be applied to clay at many stages of dryness, including bisque ware in some cases. Slips, on the other hand, are usually applied to a leather-hard surface.

Since various clays shrink and fire at different rates, the slip or engobe should be chemically compatible with the clay used to make the form.

While most slip formulations are applied to leather-hard ware, some work well at any stage of dryness, from moist to bisque (but take care applying it to the fragile stage of greenware).

Both slips and engobes can be used for sgraffito, inlay, slip trailing, stenciling, and texture brushwork, techniques that are explained on pages 90 to 97. Slips and engobes are also used in a functional way. Some transparent glazes look rather murky on a dark clay body. A white background of slip, applied first, allows the vibrant colors of a transparent glaze to show true on the ware.

The method you use to apply the material—with a brush, for example— will be apparent after firing. Vary the consistency of the slip or engobe to tweak the look. A thinner slip yields a smoother, more even finish. Use a thicker slip to show confident brush strokes.

Traditional slips and engobes fire to a matte finish, similar to bare bisque ware. If you wanted a shiny finish, first fire the applied slip or engobe, then apply a temperature-compatible clear glaze after taking the piece out of the kiln, and fire the piece yet again.

Be aware that applying a noncompatible slip or engobe often yields disastrous results. If you put a low-fire slip on a high-fire clay body, you'll end up with a soupy mess. Alternatively, firing a high-fire slip on a low-fire clay body will probably cause the slip to crack off.

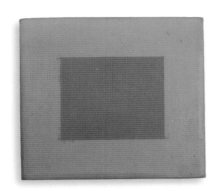

Terra sigillata, the middle layer in this jar, is a slip made of fine clay particles. The top and bottom layers are discarded.

TERRA SIGILLATA is a type of slip that contains only the finest particles of clay. Most often used to achieve a deep satin finish by *burnishing* (see page 98), it can also be applied and fired for a soft waxy surface.

Terra sigillata is made by combining clay and water, then adding a *deflocculant* to help the finer particles separate from the heavier ones. The mixture rests for at least 24 hours so that it separates into three parts. The top is excess water, the bottom contains the heavier clay particles, and the middle layer contains the finer particles, or terra sigillata. The unwanted water is retrieved using a siphon. The terra sigillata is siphoned off as well. Once the terra sigillata is collected, the bottom layer can be discarded (see the recipe on page 123).

As with other slips, terra sigillata can be made in an array of colors. Traditionally, its colors mimic the clay body it came from, so you can have shades of black, red, or white. Small amounts of colorants can be added to a white base to create subtle variations. Terra sigillata is applied to bone-dry clay by either dipping the form into it or brushing it on (see pages 111 and 113). To retain its natural lustrous sheen, terra sigillata should be fired at a low temperature (usually not higher than cone 04; see page 117 to learn more about pyrometric cones). After firing, you can add glazes on top of it.

UNDERGLAZE is a mixture of fine clay particles and colorants formulated to use on clay at any stage of dryness or on bisque-fired ware. Although it's usually applied under a clear glaze, it's sometimes applied on top of an opaque base glaze; majolica decoration is a good example of this treatment. Underglaze can be used on any type of clay, and many underglazes can be fired to virtually any temperature.

This versatile medium is similar to paint. You can use it to draw a bird or any other motif. You can mix underglazes of various colors to create new colors, such as combining yellow and blue to make green. (Because commercial underglaze formulas are so inexpensive and reliable, most ceramic artists choose to purchase them rather than mixing their own.) Unlike glaze, the color of unfired underglaze closely resembles the color it will be after the piece is fired.

Although underglaze, slips, engobes, and terra sigillata don't require glazing, a coating of clear or transparent glaze can accentuate the look and feel of the surface, as well as make the form safe for food. A clear glaze adds shine and deepens the colors of both the underglaze and clay.

METHODS

The materials that you learned about on pages 90 to 92 can be used in a tremendous number of ways. Some of the most well known are explained here: sgraffito, inlay, slip brushwork, slip trailing, stenciling, burnishing, and underglaze painting.

While the instructions that follow just scratch the surface of what's possible, you'll learn enough to get started in surface decorating. You can experiment with these techniques using the square plate project on page 100.

Once you know the basics, you can continue to develop your skills in techniques that you find most appealing. You may even end up applying several techniques to a single form, for a complex, one-of-a-kind piece.

Consider surprising a viewer with surface detail on the back or bottom of a piece. Decorate the back first so you won't mar the front.

Manufacturers produce underglazes in many forms: liquid, pencil, chalk, and dry palette (similar to the palette for watercolor paints). Each medium poses special challenges. Underglaze can be brushed, spattered, sponged, drawn, or trailed (squeezed in a thin line) onto a form. You can use it in thin coats like watercolors, or apply it in thick layers for opaque coverage. Unlike slip, underglaze doesn't retain any marks from the application method, nor enhance surface texture. In liquid form, the consistency of underglaze resembles heavy cream. It coats the surface without interfering with any of the clay's textural detail.

Sgraffito

Etching a surface is a great way to create bold, graphic designs. You aren't carving directly into the clay with this technique; instead, you work into a coating that you've applied to a leather-hard piece. The coating, which is left to dry before you start working on the surface, can be a slip, engobe, or underglaze (see pages 90, 91, and 92).

Any type of clay is suitable for sgraffito, but the technique is most effective with high-contrast colors, such as white slip on red clay or black slip on white clay.

Start the process by dipping a wide paintbrush into a slip, engobe, or underglaze. Choose a material that's compatible with the clay used to make the form. The most commonly used material is slip, so the rest of these instructions will use this material to describe the process.

Evenly distribute the liquid on the surface of the ware.  Visible brush marks are acceptable, although you don't want the slip so thick that the surface has defined ridges. (Use an underglaze, rather than slip, if you don't

want any surface texture at all.) Let the slip dry. Brush on a second layer of slip to ensure opaque coverage.

Set the form aside until it's dry to the touch. Lightly sketch your design on the plate, using a soft-lead pencil. A needle tool scratches the surface, so don't use it unless you're confident or want a spontaneous design.

Carve into the surface along the applied design lines, using the ball stylus and a variety of the metal loop tools. 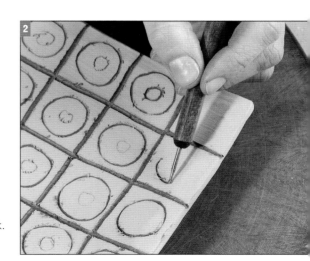 Your goal is to scrape off the slip to expose the surface of the clay underneath. Use tools of different widths to add interest to your lines. Keep in mind that the marks you make will shrink as the clay dries. For example, a needle tool makes a line so thin it may almost disappear. A ball stylus, on the other hand, has a wider tip that's more appropriate for line work.

Metal loop tools are perfect for carving out larger shapes.

The slip is too dry if it chips. If you make a mistake, you'll have to sponge off the slip and start over. When you're satisfied with your work, bisque fire the piece. Now you can apply a clear glaze, if desired, and proceed to the second firing.

Inlay

Here's an opportunity to turn a design into a form. When it reaches the leather-hard stage, you'll carve into the clay surface and then fill the areas with a contrasting-color slip or engobe. Scraping away the excess slip on the surface reveals the inlaid pattern.

First sketch your design on the form with a soft-lead pencil or a needle tool. This allows you to play around with design and composition before starting carving. For carving, choose the ball stylus tools or metal loop tools to carve in a design 1/8 inch (3 mm) deep. **3**

Next, fill the incised lines by brushing a layer of slip of a contrasting color into the carved areas. **4** Slip contains quite a bit of water so it has a higher shrinkage rate than the piece you're working on. You don't want to fill the carved area with one thick pass of slip because the slip will shrink and possibly crack while drying. Instead, apply several thinner layers and let each one dry to the touch before adding the next. Once the slip level is even with the surface, let it dry to the leather-hard stage.

Scrape off the excess slip with a rounded rib. **5** When scraping off the excess clay, choose a rib best suited for the clay body. If the clay has a lot of grog, for example, use a stiff rubber rib. Metal ribs will bring grog to surface, creating a very rough texture undesirable for food ware. This will uncover the inlaid design.

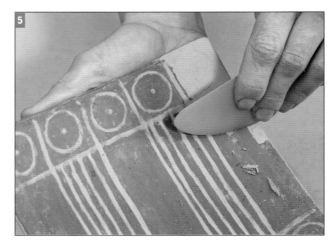

Slip Texture

Surface texture is easy to create with slip; its fluid consistency makes it ideal to manipulate on a leather-hard form. Your piece will have rich, luxurious brush strokes if you paint on the slip with a stiff brush. But that's not the only way to add texture: You can also pour slip onto a form and then push it around with your fingers to make a softly undulating surface.

The following instructions feature finger-painted concentric squares and a brush-applied spiral. You can, however, create any desired motif, and there are many ways that you can create texture with slip.

Thin slip contains a lot of moisture that could make the work slump, even though it's leather hard. Your best bet when covering a large area is to use a thicker slip that contains less water. A good rule of thumb is to use slip the consistency of cake batter.

To make concentric squares, you will have the most control by holding the plate in one hand. Brush the piece with a ⅛-inch-thick (3 mm) layer of slip. Turn the plate slowly and smoothly while using your fingers to spread the slip over the surface. **6** If working on a plate or bowl, also spread the slip around the rim.

To create slip texture on both sides of a form, let the slip dry thoroughly before flipping the piece over. To make a spiral texture, place the piece on the banding wheel and brush on a layer of slip. Turn the wheel with a steady motion and, starting at the rim, drag a paintbrush **7** or your fingers toward the center.

When the slip is bone dry, bisque fire your work and then apply glaze if desired.

Slip Trails

Lines drawn with slip add wonderful dimension to a form's surface. Slip trailing is an ideal technique for a loose, gestural design.

For this technique, you use a slip applicator to apply the lines to a leather-hard piece. Slip applicators come in a variety of shapes and sizes so that you can do an array of line work. Some of the fancier models can be quite costly. Start with a basic one that has a single applicator tip.

Underglaze can also be used in place of slip. Since underglaze has a thinner consistency, use a very narrow-tipped applicator to control the flow.

The drawn lines can't be erased, so this technique requires a confident hand. (To repair a mistake, let the piece dry and then sand off the error.)

Place the piece on a banding wheel. Extend your arm so it's comfortable and free to move across the surface. Support the forearm with your opposite hand, if desired. Hold the tip of the slip applicator over the piece, less than $\frac{1}{16}$ inch (1.6 mm) from the surface. Don't let it touch the piece,

as this may gouge the clay and clog the applicator. Hover the tip over the plate as you gently squeeze out the slip and draw your design.

Make your strokes in an outward motion. You can experiment with line thickness by altering the speed and flow of the line. A quicker stroke that emits less slip produces a thinner line. A slower stroke produces a thicker line. Try altering the line thickness to vary your design. When you're finished with the applicator, flush the tip with water and run a thin wire through it to clean out the hole.

When the work is leather hard, bisque fire it and then apply glaze, if desired.

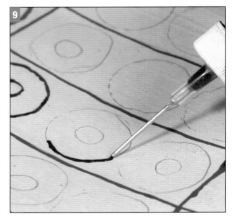

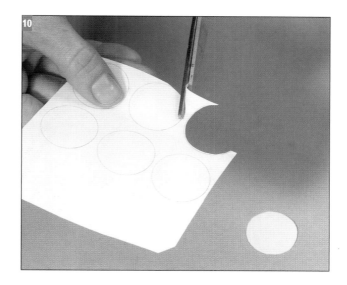

Stencils

Want to repeat the same image several times on a form, or to block slip or underglaze from parts of the surface—without painstaking hand drawing? Then stencils are just the things for you. A stencil can be a leaf, a scrap of lace, or even a shape cut out of copy paper or vellum. Placed on the surface of a leather-hard piece, a stencil acts as a mask that shields parts of the surface when you apply slip or underglaze.

Almost any flat shape is suitable as a stencil, but consider shapes that create bold designs, which effectively use negative space. The best found objects won't absorb slip or underglaze and can be peeled off the surface without crumbling or shredding. A stencil doesn't have to be solid. In fact, holes will add more interest.

To mask straight lines, all you have to do is apply a low-tack masking tape.

To create your own design, draw it on copy paper and then cut it out with scissors or a mat knife. **10** Vellum is an ideal material because it's a durable, plastic-like paper that doesn't absorb

water. A mat knife, particularly if it has a swivel head, can cut into corners and trim precise, delicate lines.

Use your finger to hold the stencil on the surface of a leather-hard piece while painting the surface with a brush dipped in a fluid slip or underglaze in a color that contrasts with the clay form. **11** Direct your strokes away from the edges of the stencil to prevent the medium from leaching underneath. Apply two thin coats. Don't worry if the slip or underglaze covers the stencil.

When the medium is dry, carefully lift off the stencil to reveal the design. **12** When the work is leather-hard, bisque fire it and then apply glaze, if desired.

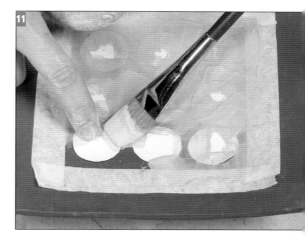

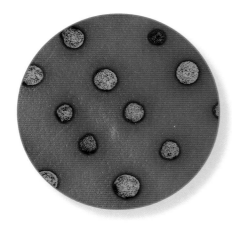

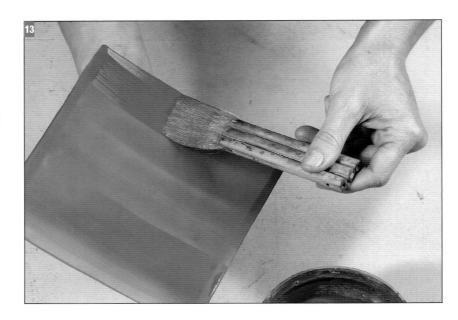

Burnished Surfaces

Burnishing compresses particles of clay so that the surface is smooth, shiny, and doesn't readily absorb moisture. Although this is a labor-intensive process, the rich, deep gleam of a finished piece is well worth the effort. Consider burnishing as an alternative to glazing a piece.

Primitive artists burnished ware that was used for food and liquids. These days, burnishing isn't recommended for surfaces that will be in direct contact with food or liquid.

Prepare a batch of terra sigillata (see page 91) while letting a clay piece become bone dry. It needs to be at this stage so that the clay absorbs a thick layer of terra sigillata. Run a soft rib over the surface when it's stiff, if necessary, to make it smooth. (A smooth surface is important, so you may not want to burnish a piece made from clay that has a lot of grog in it [see page 11].)

Particles of terra sigillata are so fine that they quickly fall to the bottom of a container. Make sure the particles are completely mixed before you begin, and stir them frequently between applications. Brush a thick, even layer of the terra sigillata, in one direction only, over the surface of a piece. **13** When the terra sigillata is dry to the touch, it's ready to be burnished.

Decide if you'll use a smooth stone, the back of a spoon, a piece of thin plastic, or just your bare finger to polish the surface. Experiment with different tools to see which one works best for you. Starting wherever desired, rub your tool of choice over the surface. **14** Apply moderate pressure.

When you've worked over the entire surface one or more times, you can consider the burnishing finished. Or, for more depth, you can add several layers of terra sigillata, burnishing between each coat to achieve the smoothest surface. Fire the finished piece.

Fired underglaze has a flat matte finish. You may leave it bare or cover it with a clear or transparent glaze. Not only does the clear coating add more surface sheen, it significantly deepens, or *saturates*, underglaze colors and even bare clay itself.

Underglaze Application

Underglazes change the color of the clay surface. You can apply one even layer of color over your entire piece, or brush on several to create a narrative painting. Experiment with many colors and various brushes to give your piece depth and personality.

Make sure that the products you select have a firing temperature that's compatible with the clay piece. When using underglaze for painterly effects, strive for layers of color to create dimension.

Experiment with the consistency of the underglaze: Water it down to achieve a translucent watercolor effect, or apply it straight from the jar for a thicker, opaque appearance. Two to three coats may be necessary for complete opaque coverage.

Start your decoration on a piece by drawing your design onto the surface, using a soft-lead pencil. Paint the larger shapes with an overall color. **15**

Now add other colors on top, for detail and dimension. **16** Additional details can be drawn on with underglaze crayons or pencils. Although underglaze can be applied to greenware or bisque ware, the crayons and pencils are easier to use on bisque ware. Finish the piece by firing to a suitable temperature for the clay.

Project: **Square Plate**

The open surface of a plate is a terrific canvas for experimenting with the decorative techniques explained on pages 89 to 90. In fact, to prepare for your surface decoration explorations, you could make several identical forms, called multiples. It's easy to make them by using a template and production methods, as explained here.

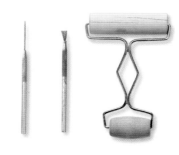

▲ **Tools**
Needle tool, scoring tool, pony roller

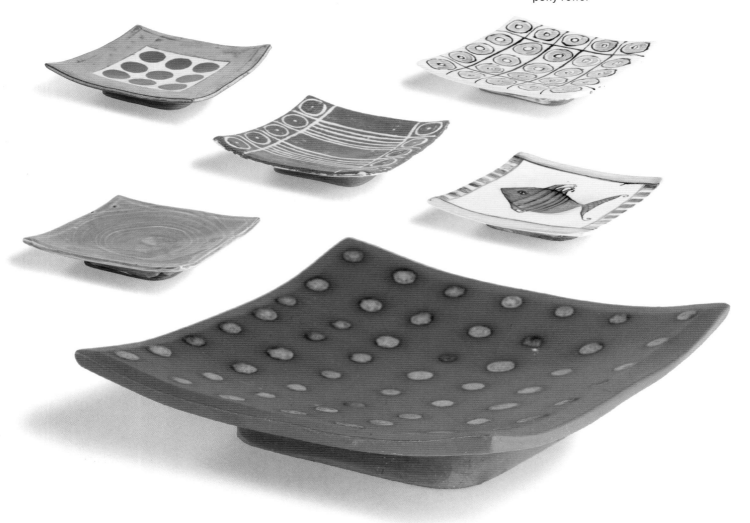

RELATED TECHNIQUES

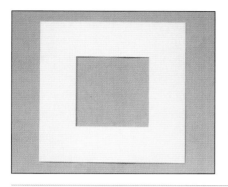

1 Make a 6-inch-square (15.2 cm) template with a 3-inch-square (7.6 cm) hole in the center. Roll a slab ¼ inch (6 mm) thick and large enough for the number of plates that you want to make.

▶ **Tip:** Utilitarian objects should be substantial enough for usage but be light enough to hold comfortably.

2 Make the desired number of squares from the slab by cutting around the perimeter of the template with the needle tool. You need one square for each plate. Still using the needle tool, lightly sketch the template's inside square on each square clay shape. This marks the position for the plate's foot. Store the shapes under a thin plastic sheet to keep them moist until you're ready to work on each one.

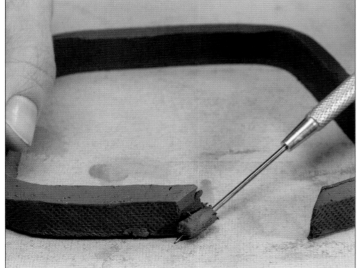

3 To form the foot (base for the plate to stand on), cut a ½ x 8-inch strip (1.3 x 20.3 cm) for each plate. Cut both of the ends of each foot at opposite mitered angles with the needle tool. Move the plate shape to a small ware board, wrong side up, and use a scoring tool to score a ¼-inch-wide (6 mm) line along the drawn line. Stand the foot so the side to be attached is facing up. Score this area, and apply a small amount of slip on it and along the scored line on the back of the plate.

▶ **Tip:** You can add interest to the foot by using stamped impressions or cutting out shapes.

4 Think about the way you'll make multiple plates. You might want to score all of the feet and face shapes at the same time, then slip and join everything at once, and so on. This and the remaining steps explain the process for one plate; adapt them as desired. Place together the slipped edge of a foot and a face. Place a line of small coils of moist clay along the entire seam along the outside of the foot. Fuse this coil until it disappears. Reinforce the interior of the seam in the same way.

5 Run a pony roller along the edges of the underside of the plate. This will taper and soften the edges. It may displace some of the clay, creating an organic edge for the rim. Run your finger along the edge of the rim to smooth the edge, if needed.

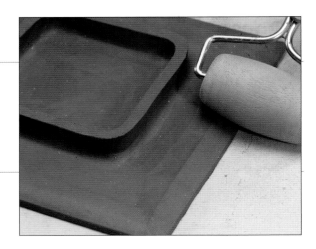

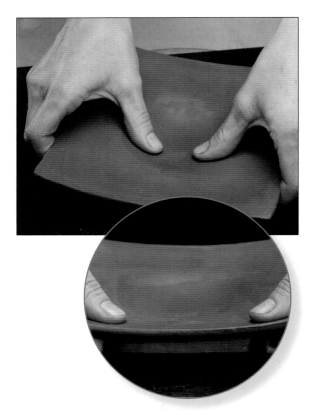

Make all of the edges the same height and ensure the center is even.

6 Set aside the plate to dry to the stiff stage, and then turn it right side up. If necessary, smooth the rim of the plate with your fingers or a damp chamois cloth. Place the plate on a bat or small ware board, and then set both on a banding wheel or lazy Susan. Press down on the center of the plate with both of your thumbs. As you press down, gently pull up two opposite sides of the rim with your fingers so that they're slightly curved. Rotate the piece and repeat this process. Cover the plate with a thin plastic sheet to keep it moist until you're ready to experiment with one of the surface decoration methods. Apply surface decoration to the plate, and fire it as desired. The set of finished plates shown on page 100 was adorned with the surface decoration techniques explained on pages 89 to 99, and finished with various glaze applications.

▶ **Tip:** Plates and other flat objects tend to warp, so carefully place the plate on a ware board to dry, and try not to misshape it.

Surface Treatment Gallery

Lana Wilson
Altar with Drawer, 2001

14 x 11 x 4½ inches (35.6 x 27.9 x 11.4 cm)
Hand-built white stoneware; stamped words, texture; dry
glaze; electric fired
Photo by artist

Barry W. Gregg
Four for the Road, 2007

24 x 9 x 9 inches (61 x 22.9 x 22.9 cm)
Hand-built stoneware; underglaze and glaze;
electric fired
Photo by Walker Montgomery

Nancy Selvin
Still Life with Red Bowl, 2004

26 x 48 x 6 inches
(66 x 121.9 x 15.2 cm)
Hand-built terra cotta; underglaze,
slip cast, screened underglaze text,
underglaze pencil; electric fired
Photo by Steve Selvin

Paul Frehe
Shazam! TV Teapot, 2007

9 x 6 x 2 inches (22.9 x 15.2 x 5.1 cm)
Hand-built, pinched white earthenware; laser decal, glazes, under-
glazes; electric fired
Photo by Steve Mann

Patrick Coughlin
Barn Butterdish, 2006

6½ x 7½ x 3½ inches (16.5 x 19 x 8.9 cm)
Slab-built, extruded, press-molded earthenware;
silk-screen transfer, low-fire glazes, terra sigillata; electric fired
Photo by artist

Jessica Kreutter
Clown Cars, 2006

7 x 7 x 4 inches (17.8 x 17.8 x 10.2 cm)
Earthenware; low-fire lithium glaze, slip, com-
mercial glaze; electric fired; post-fired assembly
Photo by artist

Cynthia Lee
Zinnia I, 2007

5 x 3⅜ inches (12.7 x 8.6 cm)
Clay, plaster slab; underglazes, glaze, flower dipped in
slip and glaze; fired
Photo by Steve Mann

Lynne Burke
Untitled, 2005

21 x 21 x 14 inches (53.3 x 53.3 x 35.6 cm)
Hand-built stoneware; cast, sculpted faces, im-
pressed leaves, slips; electric fired
Photo by Walker Montgomery

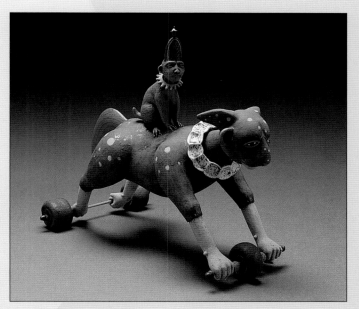

Melody Ellis
Tricycle, 2006

8 x 5½ x 9½ inches (20.3 x 14 x 24.1 cm)
Pinched, hollowed earthenware, carved; terra
sigillata, underglaze/slip, glaze, black copper oxide
wash; electric fired; post-fired assembly
Photo by artist

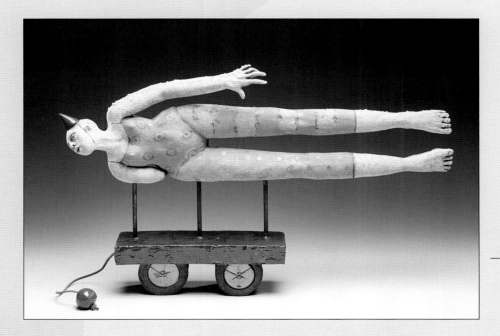

Nancy Kubale
Cirque, 2006

12 x 20 x 6 inches (30.5 x 50.8 x 15.2 cm)
Slab, coiled stoneware clay; oxides, underglaze,
terra sigillata, glaze, underglaze pencil; multi-fired
Photo by Robert Batey

Glazing

Behind the simple applications afforded by glazing lie some amazing chemistry and fascinating processes. Here's the general information you need to know before you take the next step with your hand-built form: why glazes work, what might go wrong, and how to execute some favorite glazing techniques.

BARE FIRED CLAY HAS A RICH, BEAUTIFUL SURFACE on its own, but glazing may add just the finishing touch your work needs. After you've hand-built a piece, and perhaps decorated the surface and bisque fired it, you're ready to apply a liquid that, upon firing, yields a glasslike surface that permanently fuses to clay.

Although there are some glazes that can be used on greenware, most are applied to bisque ware. You can buy these raw ingredients to weigh and mix your own glaze (see Recipes on page 122), or purchase prepared products. The materials that make the magic, and the basics of some techniques, are described in this section.

■ MATERIALS

The qualities of glazes—transparency, degree of shine, color, and texture—are the result of the complex interaction of glaze ingredients to each other, the clay body, and firing conditions such as the kiln's temperature and *atmosphere* (the fuel-to-oxygen ratio). The decisions you make when selecting a glaze involve its chemical composition, colorants, appearance, and texture. All these terms are explained here.

All glazes require three basic components for stability: silica, flux, and alumina.

The natural colorants, from top, copper carbonate, cobalt carbonate, and red iron oxide change the finished appearance of clay.

Chemicals

Glazes can be formulated from a virtually endless combination of ingredients. Colorants, *opacifiers*, and texturizers are added for other qualities.

Silica is the primary material in a glaze. As a glass former, it's responsible for fusing the glaze to the clay surface. Two common types of glass formers used for glazes are flint and silica. Silica's high melting point (3200°F/1760°C) needs to be lowered with additives known as *fluxes*. These substances are found in the form of feldspar, lithium, magnesium, and sodium. Manufacturers have also developed formulas for *frits*, glass-derivatives, which are designed to melt at specific temperatures and also lower silica's melting point. Fluxes and frits influence the look, feel, and durability of a glaze.

Alumina is a stabilizer. Without it, the glaze would melt and run off the surface of the clay. Ball clay (see page 8) and kaolin (see page 8) are two common stabilizing materials because they contain significant amounts of alumina. Alumina also increases the opacity and hardness of a glaze.

Colorants

Oxides and carbonates color a glaze. They may also alter the texture, the opacity, or both of these characteristics in a glaze.

In addition to the natural color change, the firing temperature and atmosphere may affect the color of the glaze. Copper, for example, turns green in a common *oxidation firing* (when oxygen is allowed inside the kiln), but can turn red when processed in a reduction atmosphere (when the inside of the kiln is deprived of oxygen).

Ceramic stains are another type of colorant. Like frits and fluxes, manufacturers formulate ceramic stains to produce specific, consistent results. They're available in a wide spectrum of colors that may be mixed like paint to create even more colors. Ceramic stains are also used to color underglaze, slip, and terra sigillata.

Appearance

As you plan and build your piece, start thinking about whether it will be glazed, and what type of glaze will enhance the form or surface decoration. In addition to color and texture (see pages 7 and 10), you'll choose transparent, semiopaque, or opaque. All three types of opacity are explained here. The same white clay was used for each example.

TRANSPARENT GLAZES are similar to clear or colored glass because light passes through them so that you can see the clay surface underneath. Transparent glazes work beautifully over a bare clay body, or they may be applied over slip or underglaze. When a colored transparent glaze is applied over a textured surface, the glaze pools in recessed areas, thus highlighting the surface underneath.

SEMIOPAQUE GLAZES have a higher concentration of colorants or opacifiers (or both) than transparent glazes. Semiopaque glazes perform beautifully over a textured surface. The color and opacity is more concentrated in the recessed areas, while the raised areas are more transparent, allowing the surface underneath to show through. This additional richness and depth accentuates the textured surface.

OPAQUE GLAZES are so saturated with colorants and opacifiers that they completely cover the surface underneath. Opacifiers can change the look and feel of a glaze: they whiten the glaze and decrease the transparency. Tin and titanium are the additives most often used to create opacity in a glaze.

Texture

Glazes can range from satiny smooth to crawly and crusty. A satin, semi-gloss, or glossy glaze is appropriate for food ware. This wide range of textural variation can transcend mere functionality—glaze texture can play a prominent role in directing the mood of a piece. A bright, glossy glaze may convey a feeling of cheerful whimsy, while a dry glaze surface may carry dark nuances of neglect or decay.

Matte, rough, or crater-like glaze is best suited for sculptural work.

■ APPLICATIONS

Glazing application can be as simple as a quick dunk or as intricate as multi-layered painting. No matter how knowledgeable you become with the art of glazing, there will always be an element of surprise when you open the kiln.

Ware Preparation

Since glazing can be quite a production, you may find it more efficient to do many pieces at once. Before handling the ware, wash your hands to remove any dirt or oil residue that could transfer to the ware. You may want to put on disposable gloves to protect your hands from any potentially toxic glazes.

Next, use a damp sponge to gently wipe down the ware. **1** Rinse the sponge frequently until all signs of dust are removed. Even the cleanest studios have some dust particles in the air. When these settle on the ware, they can act as a resist, causing crawling and adherence problems (see page 114). Let the ware dry for at least an hour. Any moisture left in the clay may prevent a sufficient amount of glaze from coating the surface.

During firing, glaze gets so hot it turns into a fluid that sticks to anything it touches. So if you fire a piece with glaze on the bottom (whether on purpose or inadvertently), the piece will likely stick to the kiln shelf—permanently.

You can prevent glaze from collecting in unwanted areas by applying a *liquid wax resist.* All you need is a foam brush, which you dip in the resist (available from a ceramic supply store) and then carefully apply it to completely dry bisque ware. **2** Apply a thin layer on the bottom, where it'll touch a kiln shelf. Apply the wax only where you want it because only a kiln firing will remove it.

If you're using a glaze that tends to run, apply the wax up onto the side of the pot about ½ inch (1.3 cm) from the bottom. Immediately rinse your brush when you're finished. Don't use it for any other purpose. If the wax dries on your brush, melt it off in boiling water.

Let the wax dry completely (it'll take about an hour) before glazing. If any glaze slops on the waxed areas, it'll just sit on the surface until you wipe it off with a damp sponge.

Glaze Preparation

After your bisque ware has been prepared, you're ready to pick the glaze. The glazing process always involves some suspense, but you can control the results by considering two factors: the firing temperature and function of the piece.

GLAZE AND CLAY NEED TO HAVE COMPATIBLE FIRING RANGES. Let's say you forget this guideline, brush a low-fire glaze on a piece made from a clay that *matures* at a high temperature, and then place the piece in a kiln that you fire to a high temperature. When you open the kiln after the firing, the low-fire glaze will have melted off the pot and onto everything around it. On the other hand, if a high-fire glaze is fired at a low temperature, the piece it's on will be covered with a bubbly, crusty surface. This result may be fantastic on a sculptural form, but it would be a catastrophe on a functional piece.

THE FUNCTION OF A PIECE DETERMINES THE GLAZE. You have the liberty of adorning a sculpture with any glaze that speaks the voice of your piece. Functional ware, however, requires more careful thought. Choose a glaze that will be pleasing to touch. A satiny finish is soft enough for a handle and still provides enough traction to ensure a good grip. A bowl coated with a glossy finish may offer irresistible appeal to the hand of its user.

Once you decide on the type of glaze to use, read the label to see if it contains any dangerous ingredients. Toxic glazes always need to be handled with care and should only be applied to nonfunctional work. Always check to make sure the glaze is food safe before applying it to a piece that will come in contact with food or drink. Wear gloves and a respirator when applying toxic glaze to a form.

When you've chosen an appropriate glaze, stir it until it's smooth and lump free. A drill with a mixer attachment is ideal for a large amount of glaze that's kept in a bucket. Smaller containers of glaze can be stirred with a handheld mixer or even a recycled chopstick. **3**

Pour the glaze through a sieve to eliminate any excessive lumps. Most glazes should have the consistency of buttermilk. If the glaze is too thick, gradually add a bit of water until it reaches the proper consistency. If the glaze is too thin, allow it to settle completely and then carefully scoop some water off the top.

Glazes have a finite shelf life. Most will last at least a year, but some undergo chemical changes faster. If you suspect any alterations, test-fire a sample prior to using it on an important piece.

Patina

Clay, like wood, can be stained to enhance its natural beauty. A patina is simply a wash of color that's applied to bisqued clay to enrich its bare surface. It looks nice on smooth clay but performs best on texture, where it really highlights the detail.

To apply a patina solution, you'll need a paint brush and a sponge. A patina solution can be easily mixed by volume (follow the recipe on page 123).

Paint the solution over the desired area. **4** Try not to dip the brush past the ferrule (the metal band that connects the bristles to the handle). If the pigment collects there, it's very difficult to remove and can leach out to contaminate other mediums you might dip the brush in.

Let the patina dry for at least an hour before you wipe off excess solution from the raised areas. **5** Use a damp sponge that's frequently rinsed in a bucket of water. Always wipe with a clean area of the sponge.

Patina stands alone beautifully, but a clear or transparent glaze can be applied afterward.

Dipping is the most popular way of applying glaze to utilitarian ware and small objects.

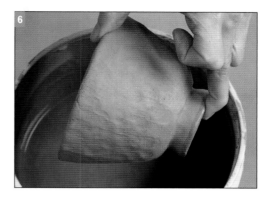

Dipped Ware

For the quickest, easiest coverage, dipping is the best method. For most glazes, one dip is usually enough to give a sufficient and even coat. You can use tongs when dipping. (Before starting, experiment to find the most comfortable, yet secure, way to hold onto the ware.) **6** Make sure your glaze is thoroughly mixed because some glazes settle quickly. Also check the consistency frequently between dips.

Submerge the piece for three seconds, gently swishing it around in the glaze to make sure it gets into any nooks and crannies. **7** Remove the piece from the glaze and carefully shake off any excess. **8** If your piece has an interior space, pour out any captured glaze. Allow the glaze to dry for a few seconds before setting it down.

If your fingers or tongs left small marks in the glaze, dot a small amount of glaze on that spot. **9** Once the glaze is completely dry, inspect your work. Use a damp sponge to remove any glaze that might cause the piece to stick to the kiln or another section of the same piece during firing (for example, a form that's fired with its lid in place.)

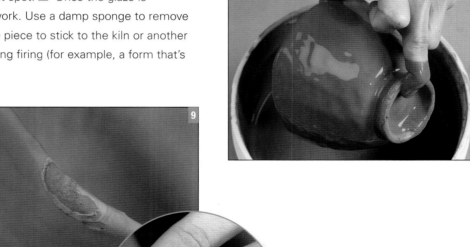

Pouring is a good alternative for ware that's too large to dip in a glaze bucket.

Poured Glaze

Use this method for a smooth, even coat of a single glaze, or to apply additional glazes to sections of a piece.

Find a shallow container large enough to hold the ware and catch glaze runoff. Place your work in the container with your hands or tongs. Scoop a cup of glaze from the glaze bucket and pour it evenly over the piece. **10** Don't let the piece sit in the collected glaze, as the ware will absorb an uneven amount of glaze.

Sometimes uneven coats of glaze are intentional. However, too much glaze can be quite problematic, especially if it settles toward the bottom of the piece. During firing, thick glaze can run onto the kiln shelf. When you're finished pouring, hold the piece just inside the glaze bucket and shake off any excess glaze before setting the piece down to dry.

If you want to also coat the interior of the piece, pour in enough glaze to coat the entire surface. **11** Tilt and rotate the ware until the entire inside is coated. **12** Wait no more than three seconds and then pour the remaining glaze back into the glaze bucket. Be careful not to let too much glaze collect in the bottom of your piece. If your piece is large enough that it takes more than three seconds to coat the inside, wipe a wet sponge around the bottom of the piece before you start. This prevents the bottom from absorbing as much glaze, so you'll have more time to swirl the glaze around the form's wall.

The easiest way to place glaze in specific areas is to brush it on.

Brushed Glaze

Brushing can be a more creative approach to glaze decoration. Spontaneous movement of a brush stroke can give character to a blank surface. **13** You can even layer brush strokes on top of a different, yet compatible, base-coat glaze. Don't make the glaze too thick.

If you're glazing a large area, use a wide brush that will cover much of the area in a few strokes. Long, thin brushes can dance across the surface of a piece, to make a gestural expression.

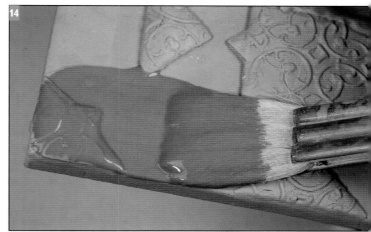

Choose a long, plump, fluffy brush that can hold a lot of glaze.

Apply two or three even coats, letting the work dry after each layer is added. The amount of glaze applied can vary depending on the individual glaze formula and the desired effects. If you're uncertain about how much to apply, test the glaze first. On a test piece, apply two coats in one area, three coats to another section, then four coats to the remaining section.

The directions for most commercial glazes recommend two to four coats. In small areas you can bypass this time-consuming process by *floating* the glaze: Saturate the brush and apply it to the surface to create a manageable pool of glaze. **14** Reload the brush frequently to float and coat one perfect, even application.

■ TROUBLESHOOTING

The results of a glaze firing can leave you feeling elated…or baffled. Even with proper knowledge and preparation, problems can occur. Here's a list of possible causes and solutions to common glaze defects.

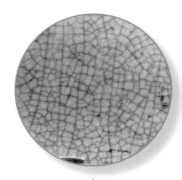

Crawling

During firing, the glaze can pull away from the clay body. You'll see an uneven surface of pools or beads, known as *crawling*. Some glazes are formulated to create this interesting texture for sculptural forms, but this wouldn't be desirable for food ware. As discussed in Ware Preparation, glaze must be applied to a clean surface. If there's dust or oil on the clay, proper adhesion cannot occur. This is one of the causes of crawling. The problem can also occur when the glaze is too thick.

Crazing

During the firing and cooling process, both clay and glaze expand and contract. When the glaze doesn't *fit* (or rest) properly with the clay body, you get *crazing*. Although this is technically considered a defect, some glazes are actually formulated to craze or *crackle*. It's a lovely aged look, but undesirable for food ware because those tiny cracks can be a haven for bacteria. To avoid crazing, choose a glaze that has a compatible firing range with the clay body. Also, prevent the thermal shock that causes crazing by never opening the kiln when the temperature inside exceeds 200˚.

Pinholing

Tiny holes or pits in the glaze surface is a defect known as *pinholing*. These imperfections are usually a result of applying too much glaze or firing too fast. In other words, you heated the kiln too quickly for the volatile gases inside to escape. In this situation the glaze doesn't have enough time to mature. In the future, try coating the ware with a thinner layer of glaze and then fire the work at a slower rate.

Blistering

Blistering causes bubbles and craters in the glaze surface. It's often a sign of a thick glaze that hasn't matured or has been *under-fired* (not heated to a high enough temperature). Blistering can also be caused by a glaze that has been *over-fired*. To prevent this defect, use a thinner glaze application and make sure the kiln is firing properly. Pinpoint any problems by using pyrometric cones (see page 117) to help monitor the accuracy of a kiln's atmospheric firing temperature.

Firing

Whether you've been working with clay for years or just a few days, it's likely that you get a thrill opening a kiln and seeing your newly fired work. Even veteran ceramists admit that there's an element of surprise in this largely scientific process.

IN ORDER FOR CLAY TO BECOME A CERAMIC MATERIAL, it must be fired. You place your clay form into a kiln with other forms and heat them to what a non-ceramist would consider very high temperatures, over an extended period of time. This time in the kiln, called firing, causes the clay to undergo a molecular change called quartz inversion, which turns the clay into a ceramic material.

In a nutshell, then, firing is about making a piece of clay harder and stronger. But there's much more to the process, because firing can also help you permanently fuse glaze to a form's surface or, at an earlier stage in the process, prepare a form to accept a glaze or other surface treatment. Firing isn't a one-step process. Depending on your piece and the desired finish, a form can undergo two or more firings. An initial firing turns a bone-dry clay form (*greenware*) into bisque ware; it's often called bisque-firing. You take these bisqued items out of the kiln, perhaps add surface decoration and finishing coatings like glaze, and then *load* them into the kiln again. This second firing (often called glaze-firing) permanently affixes the coatings to the surfaces of the pieces. Sometimes there's a third—or even more—firings to achieve the look you want.

The way that you approach firing is to a great extent determined by the type of kiln you're using. (To gain an understanding of the types of kilns, see page 22.) Most beginner—and some professional—ceramists use an electric kiln. For this reason, the process described here focuses on an electric kiln firing. At the end of this chapter, some other common firing methods are explained.

PREPARATION AND LOADING

First you need to build enough forms to fill the kiln. It's a really bad idea to run a kiln with only one piece in it because it's a waste of electricity or fuel. A full kiln also protects your ware from thermal shock, which causes surface cracks when the ware cools too quickly. (During a cool-down phase of the process, wares in the kiln gradually release the heat they absorbed when the kiln was getting hotter, thus regulating the temperature.)

Clay forms that are undergoing a first firing must be bone-dry (see page 115) when they're placed in the kiln. If one isn't dry enough, it could explode when heated. You don't want this to happen because the detritus of a problem piece can damage the kiln and the other ware.

All different types of clay can be fired together for an initial bisque-firing. (When glaze-firing, however, the clay and glazes must be fired no higher than the specific temperatures they've been formulated for.)

If you've looked inside a kiln, you're probably wondering how to load the ware because the chamber is basically just an open area. Depending on the shape and firing stage, some pieces can be *stacked* on top of one another. The rest of the work can be accommodated by inserting kiln shelves that are held in place with posts and stilts. These kiln accessories are mix and match, so you can configure them to best suit your needs. Insert shelves as you pack the kiln, staggering them for sufficient air circulation.

Large tiles or platters that have a significant bottom surface need to move freely as they shrink during a bisque firing. You can help them move around by spreading grog on the shelf wherever you want to place such a piece. Grog's sandlike particles help the ware shift along the shelf without resistance.

With greenware, it's important to allow sufficient airflow between the pieces. They can touch, but shouldn't be packed too tightly. *Crowding* interferes with even heat distribution. Start by placing larger pieces at the bottom of the kiln. Ware can be placed on top of one another, but too much weight stacked on a lower piece can cause it to break. Invert and stack plates and bowls rim-to-rim.

Ware that's coated with a raw (unfired) glaze requires extra care when the pieces are loaded for a glaze-firing. See page 109 for guidance on applying glaze to a ware. That page also explains how to coat the bottom of a piece with a liquid wax resist. This resist prevents a piece from sticking—often permanently—to a kiln shelf.

Unfired glaze is fragile, so handle the pieces carefully. Any places you disturb the glaze (even with a touch) will be visible on the piece after firing. Make sure that the pieces are spaced at least ½ inch (1.3 cm) away from the kiln walls, posts, and other work. Glaze sticks to anything it touches during the firing process.

Photo by David Gamble

■ ADDING A CONE

Leave room in your kiln for a *pyrometric cone.* This is a pyramid-shaped piece of ceramic material (sometimes a pyrometric bar is used instead) that you use to monitor the condition inside a kiln that's firing. Each cone (or bar) is designed to monitor a precise temperature over a specific length of time. When it reaches the *maturing range* (optimal conditions), the tip bends, slowly, over about 20 minutes. Information that's usually included with the box of cones you purchase gives you a general idea when it's time to start monitoring your kiln.

The cone that you put in the kiln is selected according to the firing temperature of the type of clay and glaze you have used. Look at the package that your clay came in: the manufacturer's label will usually tell you the suitable cone, as indicated by a number. Low-fire earthenware, for example, generally fires at cone 04. Cone 022 is for the lowest temperature of 1112°F (600°C). Cone 13 is for the highest temperature of 2455°F (1346°C).

Even kilns that have temperature and time-setting devices should include a cone in every firing. In fact, some kilns are equipped with a kiln sitter, which shuts off the firing when a cone bends the desired amount.

Photo by Evan Bracken

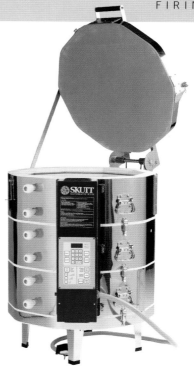

Electric Kiln. Photo courtesy of Skutt Kilns

■ THE FIRING SCHEDULE

You don't just fill a kiln with forms, flick a switch, and walk away. In order for the clay material to become ceramic—or for a glaze to fuse properly to a bisque-fired surface—the temperature of the kiln must be raised slowly, held at a peak temperature, and then lowered in a controlled fashion. This procedure, known as the firing schedule, depends on the clay body and the type of kiln. The entire firing could be an overnight process, or take several days, depending on the size of the kiln. It's most important that you follow the specific information in the kiln manufacturer's manual.

A computerized electric kiln will adjust and hold interior temperatures as programmed. With a manual kiln, however, you could be adjusting the temperature six or more times over intervals of one, four, or more hours.

A bisque-firing begins with an initial kindling: After loading the ware, you leave the kiln's lid slightly ajar and heat it at the lowest possible setting for four to six hours. This dries the greenware still more.

The temperature is usually set to rise faster during a glaze-firing, as compared to a bisque-firing, and there isn't an initial kindling. You sustain the peak temperature for a specific length of time, which is called giving the kiln a soak, to allow glaze to fully mature.

In any type of kiln firing, you always want to monitor the process. Never leave a kiln unattended. Even the most modern computerized kilns can malfunction. This malfunction can result in the kiln overheating, ruining the ware inside, the kiln itself, and even causing a fire.

■ OTHER TYPES OF FIRING

Pit firing is a simple, primitive method. Dig a hole in the ground that's large enough for the wares and combustibles like sticks, leaves, and (sometimes) dung. Ware going into the pit is often painted with terra sigillata (see page 91) and first bisqued at a very low temperature to keep the clay open (porous). The pieces are then nestled in the pit among the combustibles. When the pit is ignited, the carbon from the burning materials pass over the clay surfaces, creating random, organic patterns. A fire with flames isn't the goal. Instead, you want the pit to smolder for several hours, and then cool down enough to safely unearth the wares.

Artists who wood fire take great pride in this long, laborious process. The wood-fired kiln is typically a large, hand-built chamber that burns at least a cord of wood in a single firing. The firing can take 20 to 30 hours and requires constant monitoring. The burning wood turns to ash and is allowed to rest on the wares, often producing rich, earthy flashes of color on the surface. Such flashes are the hallmarks of the wood-firing process.

Raku is an ancient Japanese firing process that uses a low-fire reduction method to add unique surface effects

A pit for firing can easily be dug in your own yard. Choose an open site where you can safely contain the fire, and check local ordinances before digging or burning.

to bisque-fired pieces. (Reduction is a general term used to indicate the fuel-to-oxygen ratio inside the closed atmosphere of the kiln.) The gas-fueled raku kiln is typically a small one, and heats to around cone 05 in about 45 minutes, which is very quick. Once the glaze has matured, the kiln is opened. Then the glazed ware is retrieved and set in a chamber (such as a pit or metal can) full of combustibles like sawdust or newspaper. This process induces thermal shock, causing intentional cracks in the surface of some types of glazes. Once ignited, the chamber is sealed, thus allowing carbon to penetrate the bare clay and turn it black. Carbon also interacts with glazes that contain copper and creates beautiful flashes of metallic color.

Templates

GEOMETRIC VESSEL, PAGE 60

Enlarge 250%

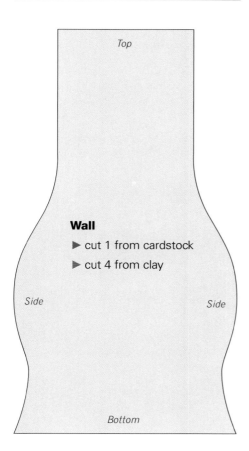

Base

▶ cut 1 from cardstock

▶ cut 1 from clay

Top

Wall

▶ cut 1 from cardstock

▶ cut 4 from clay

Side   Side

Bottom

CARVED LANTERN, PAGE 63

Enlarge 285%

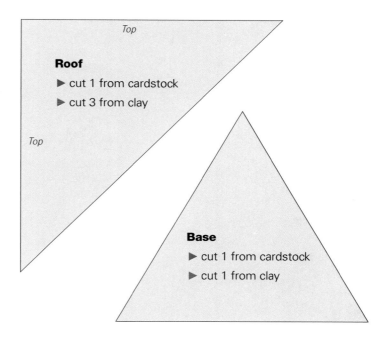

Top

Roof

▶ cut 1 from cardstock

▶ cut 3 from clay

Top

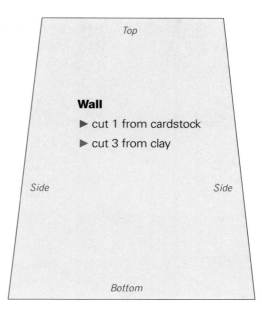

Base

▶ cut 1 from cardstock

▶ cut 1 from clay

Top

Wall

▶ cut 1 from cardstock

▶ cut 3 from clay

Side   Side

Bottom

BIRD SCULPTURE, PAGE 75

Enlarge 200%

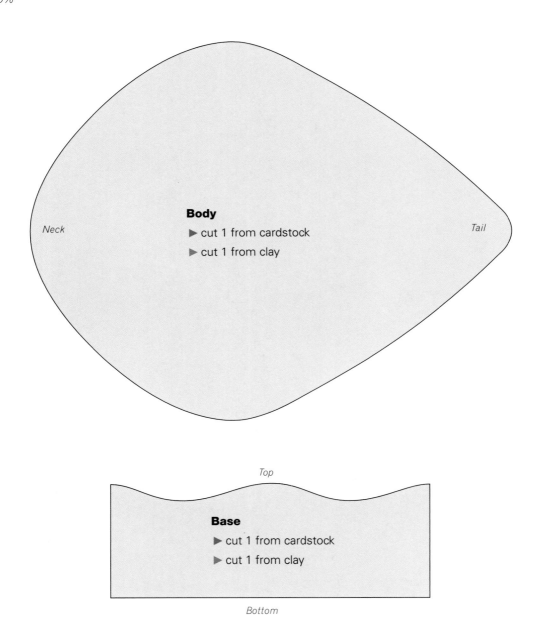

Neck

Body
► cut 1 from cardstock
► cut 1 from clay

Tail

Top

Base
► cut 1 from cardstock
► cut 1 from clay

Bottom

NESTING BOX, PAGE 79

Enlarge 200%

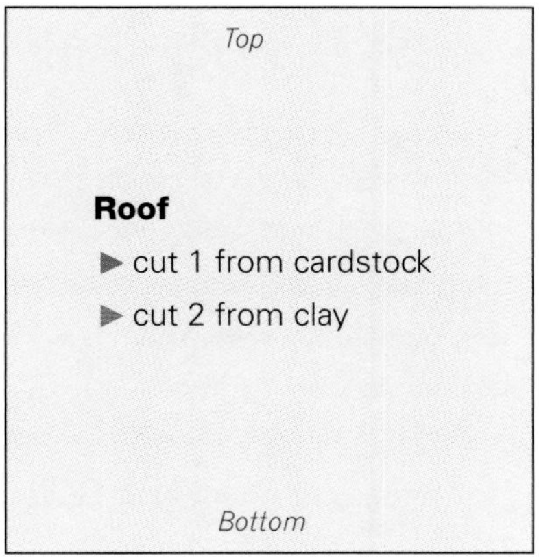

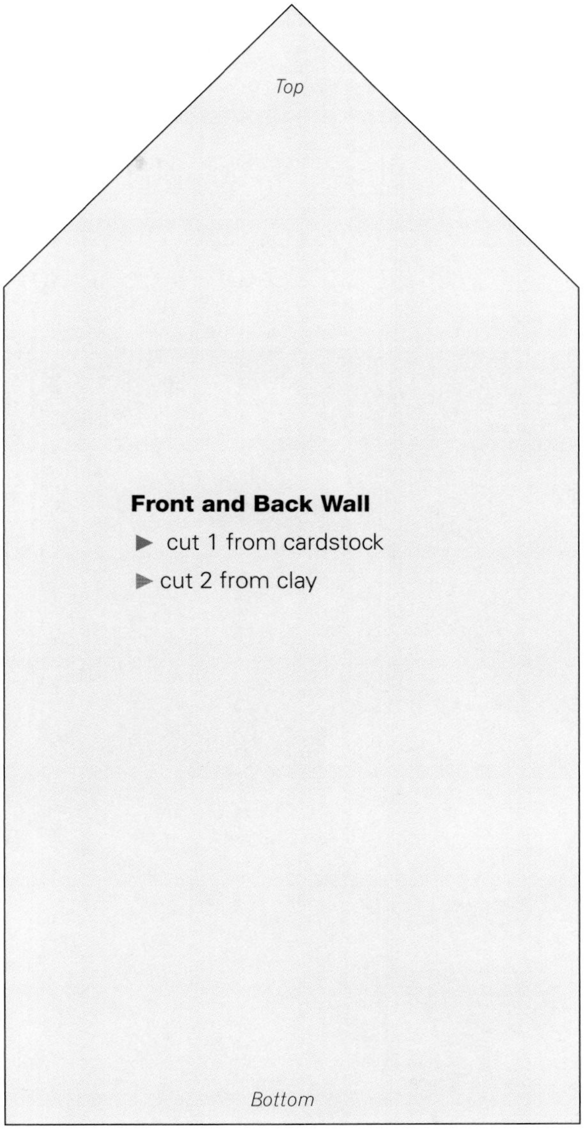

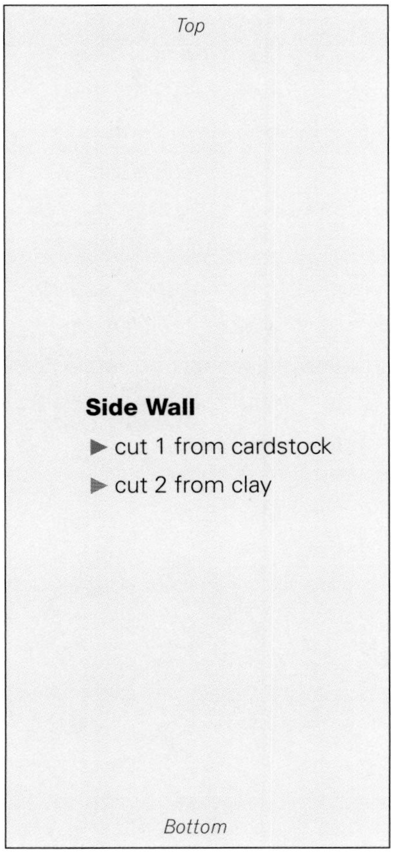

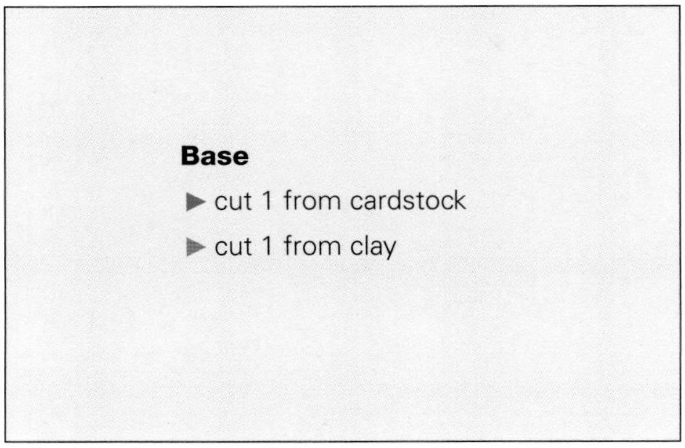

Top

Roof
► cut 1 from cardstock
► cut 2 from clay

Bottom

Top

Front and Back Wall
► cut 1 from cardstock
► cut 2 from clay

Bottom

Top

Side Wall
► cut 1 from cardstock
► cut 2 from clay

Bottom

Base
► cut 1 from cardstock
► cut 1 from clay

Recipes

Here are a few recipes to whet your appetite for mixing your own slip, base, and more. Before making a selection, note the type of ware that it's intended for, and always consider the ware's firing temperature.

With the exception of the Patina Wash and Terra Sigillata, the numbers in the ingredients are percentages of the total, which enables ceramists to mix any volume desired. Moreover, the glazes can be altered by adding recommended percentages of colorants to create an exciting palette. The ingredients of all but one of these recipes (the terra sigillata) are measured by weight.

To mix up a recipe, you'll need a scale, two buckets, a mixer, rubber gloves, and a mask or respirator. Measure the dry ingredients into a bucket and mix in enough water to achieve the consistency specified in the instructions. Pour the liquid through a sieve that's resting on the second bucket. If necessary, push the glaze through the sieve with a rubber rib. Sieve one more time. Let the contents rest for 24 hours before application to a form.

■ WHITE SLIP, CONE 04–10

Apply to leather-hard clay.

Feldspar	25.0
Kaolin (EPK)	45.0
Flint	15.0
Bentonite	10.0
Pyrophyllite	5.0
Total	100.0

Sieve and mix the ingredients to the consistency of split pea soup.

■ PATINA WASH

Apply to bisque ware.

Note: This recipe is mixed by volume.

Oxide or stain	1 part
Kaolin (EPK)	1 part
Frit 3124	1 part

Mix the ingredients to the consistency of skim milk.

■ GLAZE BASE, CONE 10

Apply to bisque ware.

Flint	25.0
Kaolin (EPK)	15.0
Feldspar	40.0
Whiting	20.0
Total	100.0

Blue: Add 2% cobalt carbonate
Green: Add 3% copper carbonate
Yellow: Add 3% red iron oxide

Mix the ingredients, adding enough water to achieve the consistency of buttermilk, and then sieve.

■ TERRA SIGILLATA, CONE 08–04

Apply to bone-dry clay.

Ball clay or red art clay	200 g
Water	840 ml
Sodium silicate	25 g

Mix the ingredients well in a large, clear glass container, and let the contents settle for 24 hours. The mixture will settle into three distinct layers. Siphon off the top layer of water and discard it. The middle layer is the terra sigillata; siphon it into a lidded container. Discard the bottom layer.

■ JACKIE'S BASE, CONE 04

Apply to bisque ware.

Gerstley Borate	38.0
Flint	42.0
Kaolin (EPK)	5.0
Nepheline syenite	5.0
Lithium	10.0
Total	100.0

Blue: Add 2% cobalt carbonate
Green: Add 3% copper carbonate and 2% red iron oxide
Yellow: Add 4% red iron oxide

Mix the ingredients, adding enough water to achieve the consistency of buttermilk, and then sieve.

■ CLEAR GLOSS GLAZE, CONE 06–04

Apply to bisque ware.

Gerstley borate	65.0
Flint	25.0
Kaolin (EPK)	10.0
Total	100.0

Blue: Add 2% cobalt carbonate
Green: Add 3% copper carbonate
Yellow: Add 4% red iron oxide

Mix the ingredients, adding enough water to achieve the consistency of buttermilk, and then sieve.

Glossary of Ceramic Terms

Alumina. A stabilizing ingredient used in glazes that have a high melting point.

Armature. A framework upon which a clay sculpture is built.

Banding wheel. A mobile turntable that enables the artist to freely turn work without handling it.

Bat. A small ware board on which work is made, transported, and dried.

Bisque ware. Ceramic material that has undergone a low initial firing process to prepare it for glazing.

Burnishing. A finishing process involving rubbing leather-hard or bone-dry clay to a polished shine.

Ceramic. Clay that has been fired to a state of chemical conversion. This process gives the material strength and permanence.

Chop mark. An imprint in clay made by a stamp with a personal signature or mark.

Clay. A type of pulverized rock combined with various organic materials. When fired, clay produces a ceramic medium.

Coddle. Raises work for access to the underside.

Coiling. A hand-building technique using rolled pieces of clay.

Cone. An elongated pyramid of ceramic material formulated to bend and melt at a specific temperature in a kiln firing.

Decal. An image made from china paints that is transferred onto a fired glazed surface and fired between cone 018 and cone 017.

Deflocculant. An additive used to lower the viscosity of a liquid medium.

Earthenware. A common clay body that matures at a low temperature range.

Engobe. A type of slip used to decorate the surface of a ceramic form.

Firing. The essential heating process that turns clay into a ceramic material. It is also used to fuse glaze and other decorative materials to the clay surface.

Fit. The adherence relationship a glaze has to a given clay body.

Flocculant. An additive used to help prevent ingredients from settling in a glaze.

Flux. Material that's used to lower the melting point of a glaze and to help it fuse to the clay body.

Foot. The base of a ceramic sculpture or utilitarian object to give lift or stability to the form.

Frit. A type of flux manufactured to melt at specific temperatures.

Glaze. A liquid mixture containing a glass former that is applied to the surface of a clay body. Once fired, it fuses to the ceramic surface, creating a permanent coating.

Greenware. An unfired clay form.

Grog. Sandlike particles of fired clay graded in various sizes. It is added to a clay body to texturize, and to decrease shrinkage and warpage.

Hand building. Constructing work in clay by pinching, coiling, or shaping and joining slabs, without the use of a potter's wheel.

Kiln. A device used to fire ceramics.

Kiln wash. A mixture of refractory materials coated on kiln furniture to protect it from melting glaze.

Mold. An object used to give clay structure or definition. It can be in the form of a slump, hump, sprig, or press mold.

Oxide. Natural material used to color clay, glaze, and other decorative mediums.

Patina. Colored wash used to stain a bare ceramic surface.

Pinching. A hand-building method of squeezing clay between fingers and thumb to form a sculpture or pot.

Plasticity. The state of damp clay, with a consistency pliable enough to be formed under pressure without cracking or breaking.

Porcelain. A white, translucent, high-fire clay body capable of reaching the highest vitreous state.

Porosity. The state of clay fired to a low temperature; pores remain open enough for water to seep through.

Pyrometer. A device used to measure the interior temperature of a kiln.

Refractory materials. Content used in clays, kiln furniture, and kiln insulation that resists high heat and melting.

Rim. The lip or top edge of a form.

Sgraffito. A decorative technique made by scratching though a layer of slip to reveal a contrasting clay color underneath.

Shrinkage. The rate clay shrinks as it dries and is fired to a given temperature.

Sieve. A wire mesh utensil to strain liquid decorative mediums.

Silica. The most common glaze ingredient that acts as a glass former.

Slabbing. A hand-building method using sheets of clay in various thicknesses to form a tile, sculpture, or pot.

Slab roller. A mechanical device used to form slabs of clay.

Slip. A liquid form of clay coated on a clay surface for decorative effects.

Sprig. A low-relief decoration taken from a small mold. It's applied to the surface of a form while both pieces are still moist.

Stain. A manufactured colorant used to tint underglaze, slip, and glaze. Stains come in a wide variety of colors and are more reliable than natural oxides.

Stoneware. A dense, high-fire clay body that's suitable for food ware.

Terra sigillata. A decorative coating of the finest clay particles, which produces a satin sheen.

Thermal shock. A process of quickly exposing a ceramic form to extreme temperature changes; can result in cracking or breaking of the surface treatment.

Undercut. Negative space cut into a form to create an overhang, to be avoided when making stamps or molds.

Underglaze. A decorative medium applied to greenware or bisque ware, used alone or under a glaze.

Viscosity. The resistence to flow in a liquid.

Vitrification. The process when a glaze or clay body is fired to a dense, nonabsorbent stage.

Ware board. A mobile, porous, flat surface used as a base when constructing and transporting work.

Warping. Unintended bending of a form caused by rapidly drying or firing a piece.

Wax resist. A coating that's applied to bisque ware to block glaze absorption.

Wedging. Kneading clay to mix it thoroughly, remove air, and improve workability.

Contributing Artists

Allen, Jill
Portland, Oregon
Page 33

Ballard, Alice
Greenville, South Carolina
Page 32

Berg, Rachel
Taconic, Connecticut
Page 84

Beyeler, Maggie Mae
Santa Fe, New Mexico
Page 85

Bidwell, Penney
Denver, Colorado
Page 32

Burke, Lynne
Hartwell, Georgia
Page 105

Calvert, Aaron
Arkadelphia, Arkansas
Page 57

Clague, Lisa
Bakersville, North Carolina
Page 44

Coughlin, Patrick
Gainesville, Florida
Page 104

Ellis, Melody
Edwardsville, Illinois
Page 105

Everett, Jennifer A.
Gorham, Maine
Page 83

Finnerty, Kathryn
Pleasant Hill, Oregon
Page 85

Fisher, Frank James
Milford, Michigan
Page 84

Fisher, Lynn
Bellaire, Michigan
Page 83

Frehe, Paul
Asheville, North Carolina
Page 104

Fritts, Debra
Roswell, Georgia
Page 42

Gentithes, Carol
Seagrove, North Carolina
Page 43

Gonzalez, Arthur
Alameda, California
Page 45

Granados, Juan
Lubbock, Texas
Page 43

Gregg, Barry W.
Decatur, Georgia
Page 103

Harper, Edwards
Asheville, North Carolina
Page 42

Jameson, Kerry
London, United Kingdom
Page 44

Kerrigan, Thomas
Tucson, Arizona
Page 32

Kieffer, Kristen
Baldwinville, Massachusetts
Page 84

Kim, Myung-Jin
Torrance, California
Page 67

Kim, Tae-Hoon
Long Beach, California
Page 67

Knutson, Barbara
Woodstock, Vermont
Page 83

Kubale, Nancy
Rutherfordton, North Carolina
Page 105

Lee, Cynthia
Barnardsville, North Carolina
Page 104

Mendes, Jenny
Chesterland, Ohio
Page 42

Nicklow, Jonathan
Evergreen, Colorado
Page 84

Nicklow, Valerie
Evergreen Colorado
Page 84

Pierantozzi, Sandi
Philadelphia, Pennsylvania
Pages 56, 57

Selvin, Nancy
Berkeley, California
Page 103

Smith, Wesley L.
Knoxville, Tennessee
Page 45

Summerfield, Liz Zlot
Bakersville, North Carolina
Page 57

Theiss, Chris
Mount Vernon, Washington
Page 67

Tirrell, Sue
Livingston, Montana
Page 56

Tisdale, James
Austin, Texas
Page 44

Walker, Holly
Randolph, Vermont
Page 45

Wee, Hong-Ling
New York, New York
Page 33

Welch, Fran
Asheville, North Carolina
Pages 45, 56

Westby, Lars
Baltimore, Maryland
Page 43

Wilson, Lana
Del Mar, California
Pages 85, 103

Wunderlich, Janis Mars
Columbus, Ohio
Page 32

About the Author

WHEN SHAY AMBER FIRST TOUCHED CLAY, she was surprised and delighted. Since that day more than 17 years ago, working with clay and teaching its mysteries have become the great passions of her life.

Shay is a ceramic artist who works exclusively with hand-built forms. She holds a degree in ceramics from Ringling School of Art and Design, completed a three-year residency at Odyssey Center for the Ceramic Arts, and received a scholarship to Watershed Center for the Ceramic Arts.

Shay owned and operated the Collective Hand Studio/Gallery where she taught classes and curated ceramic exhibitions. She lives in Asheville, North Carolina. As an active artist and teacher, her work is displayed in galleries and permanent collections nationally. To see more of Shay's work, visit her website at **www.shayamber.com**.

Photo by Craig Childs

ACKNOWLEDGMENTS

I WOULD LIKE TO THANK THE FOLLOWING PEOPLE FOR THEIR ASSISTANCE IN MAKING THIS BOOK POSSIBLE:

- My mother, **Elaine Reich**, who has given me stellar guidance and shared her grammatical expertise;
- **David Bollt**, for his ongoing patronage and many years of believing in me;
- **Mark Burleson**, for opening many doors of opportunity in my career;
- My best friend, **Tom Metcalf**, who reminded me to laugh during the toughest of times;
- **Craig Childs,** for the support, assistance, and patience that went above and beyond the call of duty; and
- My father, **Jesse Reich**, who gifted me with the ability to teach.

SPECIAL THANKS TO THE TEAM THAT HELPED MAKE THIS BOOK POSSIBLE:

Thom Gaines, Timothy Haney, Susan Huxley, Steve Mann, Kathleen McCafferty, Nathalie Mornu, Beth Sweet, Suzanne Tourtillott, Margot Wallston, Fran Welch, Chris Bryant, Jeff Hamilton, Jackie Kerr, Shannon Yokeley

Index

Shay Amber
Crossroads, 2004

18 x 11 x 4 inches (45.7 x 27.9 x 10.2 cm)
Stiff-slab, pinched, and carved earthenware;
stamp appliqué; underglaze, patina, glaze
application; cone 06
Photo by artist